E S T A T E P U

NORTHAMPTON

EARLS BARTON MOULTON HARPC

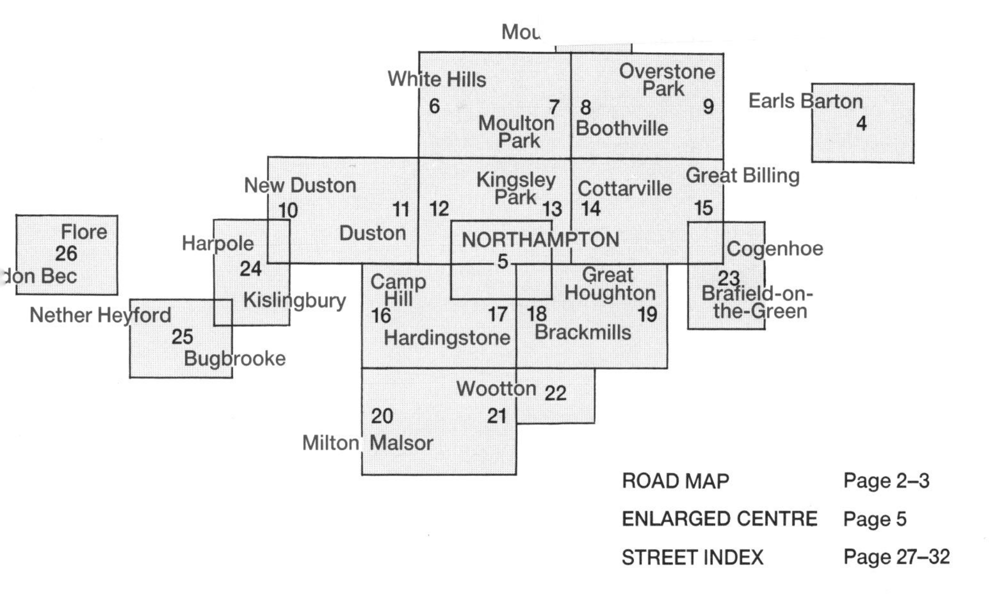

ROAD MAP	Page 2–3
ENLARGED CENTRE	Page 5
STREET INDEX	Page 27–32

Every effort has been made to verify the accuracy of information in this book but the publishers cannot accept responsibility for expense or loss caused by any error or omission. Information that will be of assistance to the user of the maps will be welcomed.

The representation of a road, track or footpath on the maps in this atlas is no evidence of the existence of a right of way.

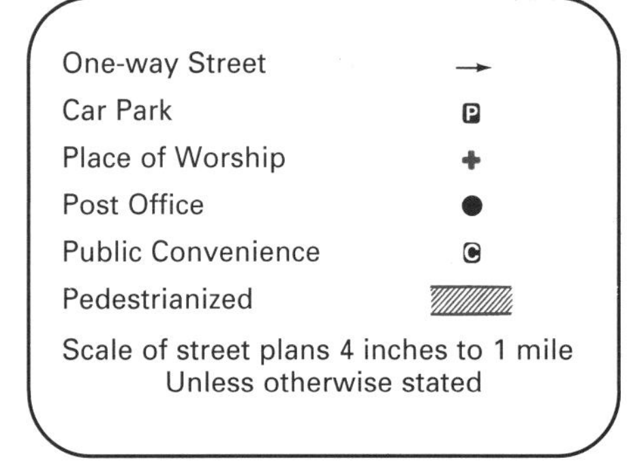

Street plans prepared and published by ESTATE PUBLICATIONS, Bridewell House, TENTERDEN, KENT, and based upon the ORDNANCE SURVEY maps with the sanction of the Controller of H. M. Stationery Office.

The publishers acknowledge the co-operation of the local authorities of towns represented in this atlas.

Estate Publications 514 B ISBN 0 86084 881 7

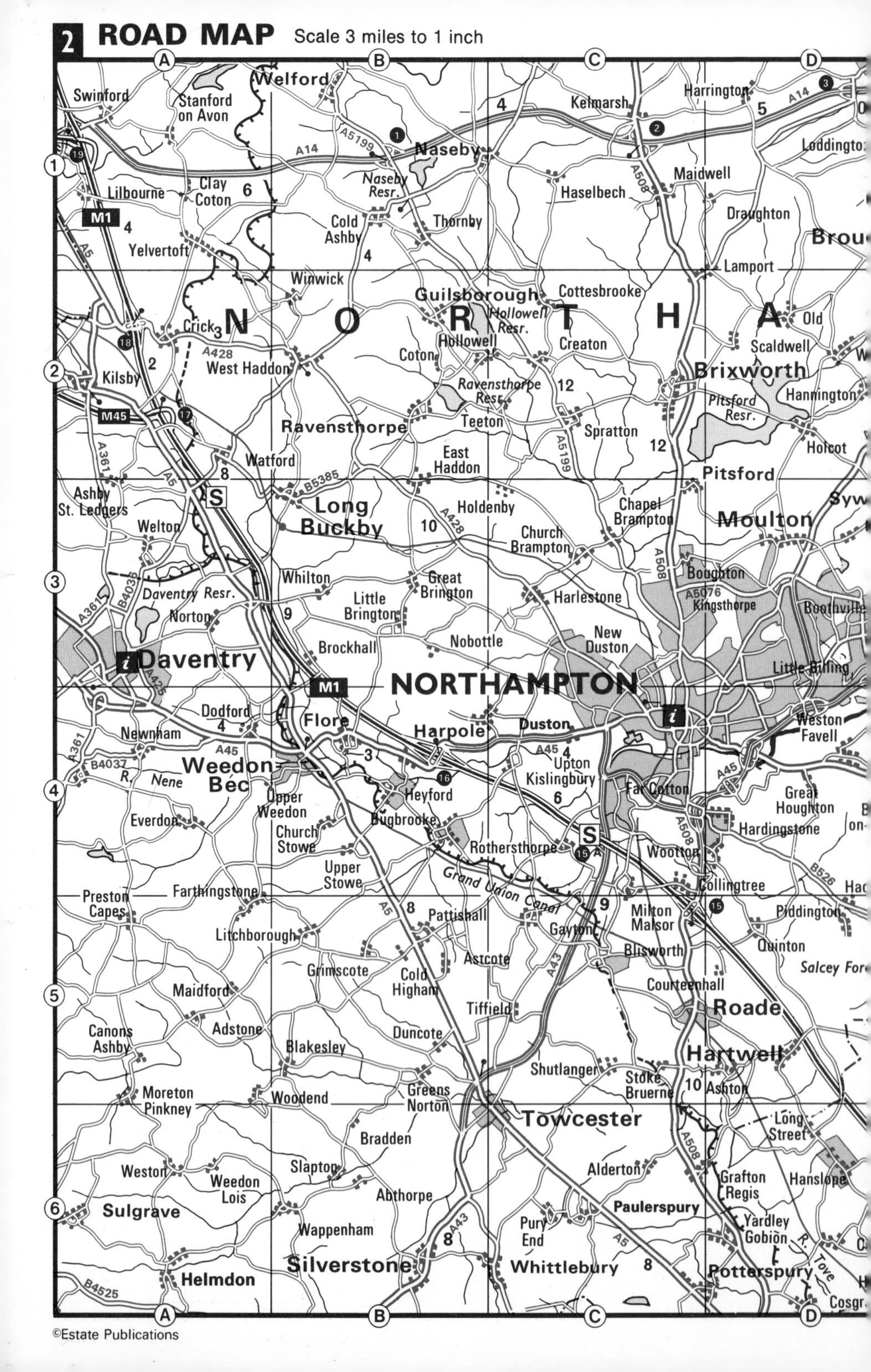

2
ROAD MAP
Scale 3 miles to 1 inch
A
B
C
D
1
2
3
4
5
6
Swinford
Stanford on Avon
Welford
Kelmarsh
Harrington
Loddington
Naseby
Naseby Resr.
A14
A5199
A508
Lilbourne
Clay Coton
M1
A5
Yelvertoft
Cold Ashby
Thornby
Haselbech
Maidwell
Draughton
Winwick
Lamport
Guilsborough
Hollowell Resr.
Cottesbrooke
Old
Crick
N
O
R
T
H
A
Kilsby
A428
West Haddon
Hollowell
Coton
Creaton
Scaldwell
Brixworth
M45
Ravensthorpe Resr.
Teeton
Spratton
Pitsford Resr.
Hannington
A361
Ravensthorpe
Watford
East Haddon
Holcot
Pitsford
B5385
Ashby St. Ledgers
Long Buckby
Holdenby
Chapel Brampton
Moulton
Welton
Church Brampton
Daventry Resr.
B4036
Whilton
Great Brington
Harlestone
Boughton
A5076
Kingsthorpe
Boothville
Norton
Little Brington
New Duston
Brockhall
Nobottle
Daventry
A425
NORTHAMPTON
Little Billing
Dodford
Newnham
Flore
Harpole
Duston
Weston Favell
A45
B4037
Weedon Bec
Upton
Kislingbury
R. Nene
Upper Weedon
Heyford
Far Cotton
Great Houghton
Everdon
Bugbrooke
Hardingstone
Church Stowe
Rothersthorpe
Wootton
Upper Stowe
Grand Union Canal
B526
Preston Capes
Farthingstone
Collingtree
Milton Malsor
Piddington
Pattishall
Litchborough
Gayton
Astcote
Blisworth
Quinton
Grimscote
Cold Higham
A43
Salcey Forest
Maidford
Courteenhall
Tiffield
Roade
Canons Ashby
Adstone
Duncote
Blakesley
Hartwell
Shutlanger
Moreton Pinkney
Woodend
Greens Norton
Stoke Bruerne
Ashton
Towcester
Long Street
Bradden
Weston
Slapton
Alderton
Weedon Lois
Grafton Regis
Hanslope
Sulgrave
Abthorpe
Paulerspury
Wappenham
Pury End
Yardley Gobion
R. Tove
Silverstone
Whittlebury
Potterspury
Helmdon
B4525
Cosgrove
S

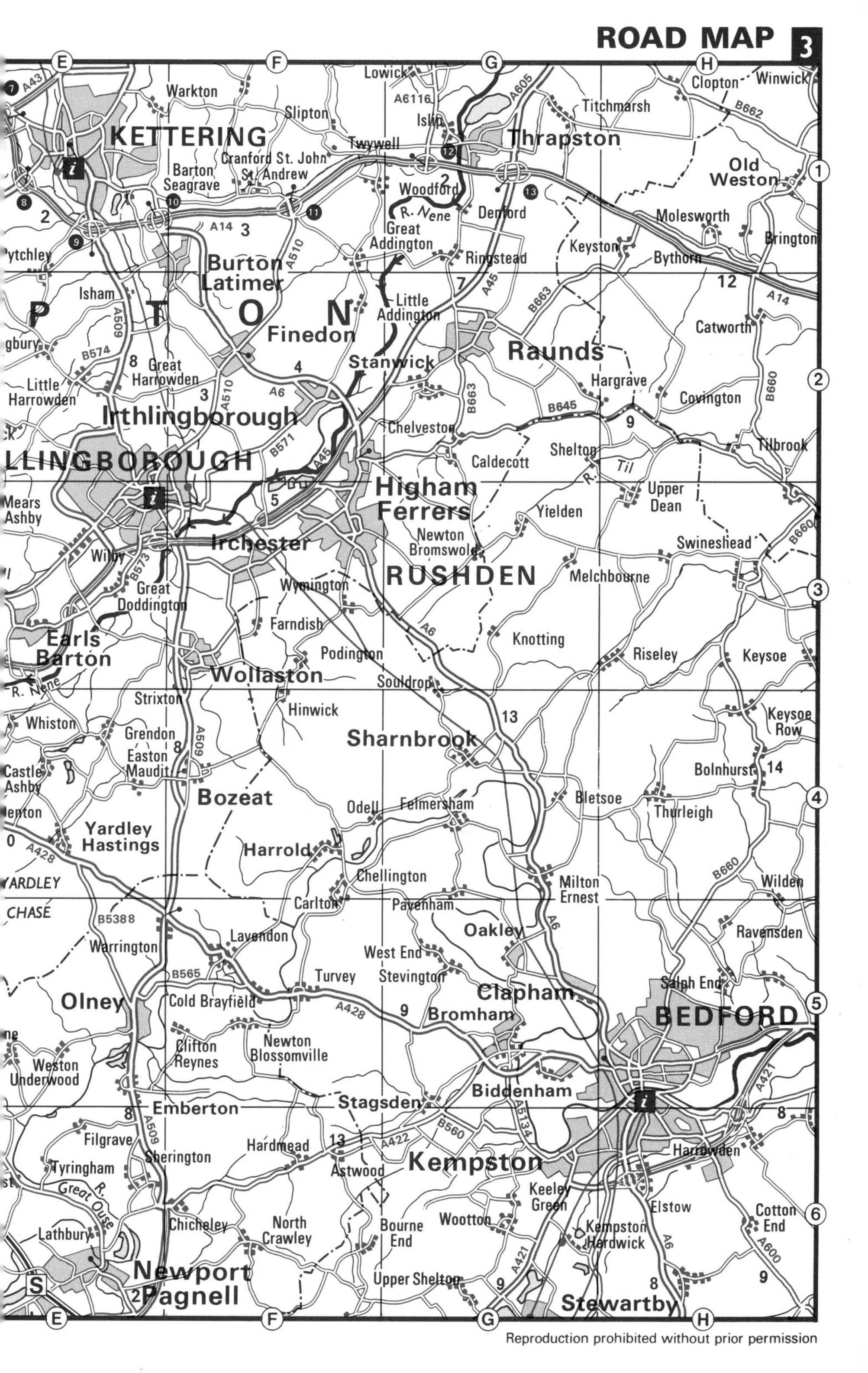
E
F
G
H
1
2
3
4
5
6
KETTERING
Warkton
Slipton
Lowick
A6116
Islip
Twywell
Thrapston
Clopton
Winwick
Titchmarsh
B662
A605
A43
Cranford St. John
St. Andrew
Barton Seagrave
Woodford
Denford
R. Nene
Great Addington
Ringstead
Old Weston
Molesworth
Brington
Keyston
Bythorn
A14
Pytchley
Burton Latimer
A510
Isham
Little Addington
A45
B663
Catworth
Finedon
Raunds
Stanwick
Hargrave
Covington
B660
Great Harrowden
Little Harrowden
B574
A509
A6
Irthlingborough
Chelveston
B645
Shelton
Tilbrook
WELLINGBOROUGH
B571
Caldecott
R. Til
Higham Ferrers
Upper Dean
Mears Ashby
Yielden
Irchester
Newton Bromswold
Swineshead
Wilby
B573
Great Doddington
RUSHDEN
Melchbourne
Wymington
Farndish
Knotting
Earls Barton
Podington
Riseley
Keysoe
Wollaston
R. Nene
Souldrop
Strixton
Hinwick
Whiston
Keysoe Row
Grendon
Sharnbrook
Castle Ashby
Easton Maudit
Bolnhurst
Denton
Bozeat
Bletsoe
Odell
Felmersham
Thurleigh
Yardley Hastings
Harrold
A428
YARDLEY CHASE
Chellington
B660
Wilden
Milton Ernest
Carlton
Pavenham
B5388
Oakley
Ravensden
Lavendon
Warrington
West End
Stevington
Turvey
B565
Salph End
Olney
Cold Brayfield
Clapham
Bromham
BEDFORD
Newton Blossomville
Clifton Reynes
Weston Underwood
Biddenham
Emberton
Stagsden
A421
Filgrave
Hardmead
B560
A422
A5134
Harrowden
Sherington
Kempston
Tyringham
Astwood
Great Ouse
Keeley Green
Elstow
Cotton End
Chicheley
North Crawley
Bourne End
Wootton
Kempston Hardwick
A600
Lathbury
Newport Pagnell
Upper Shelton
Stewartby
S

EARLS BARTON

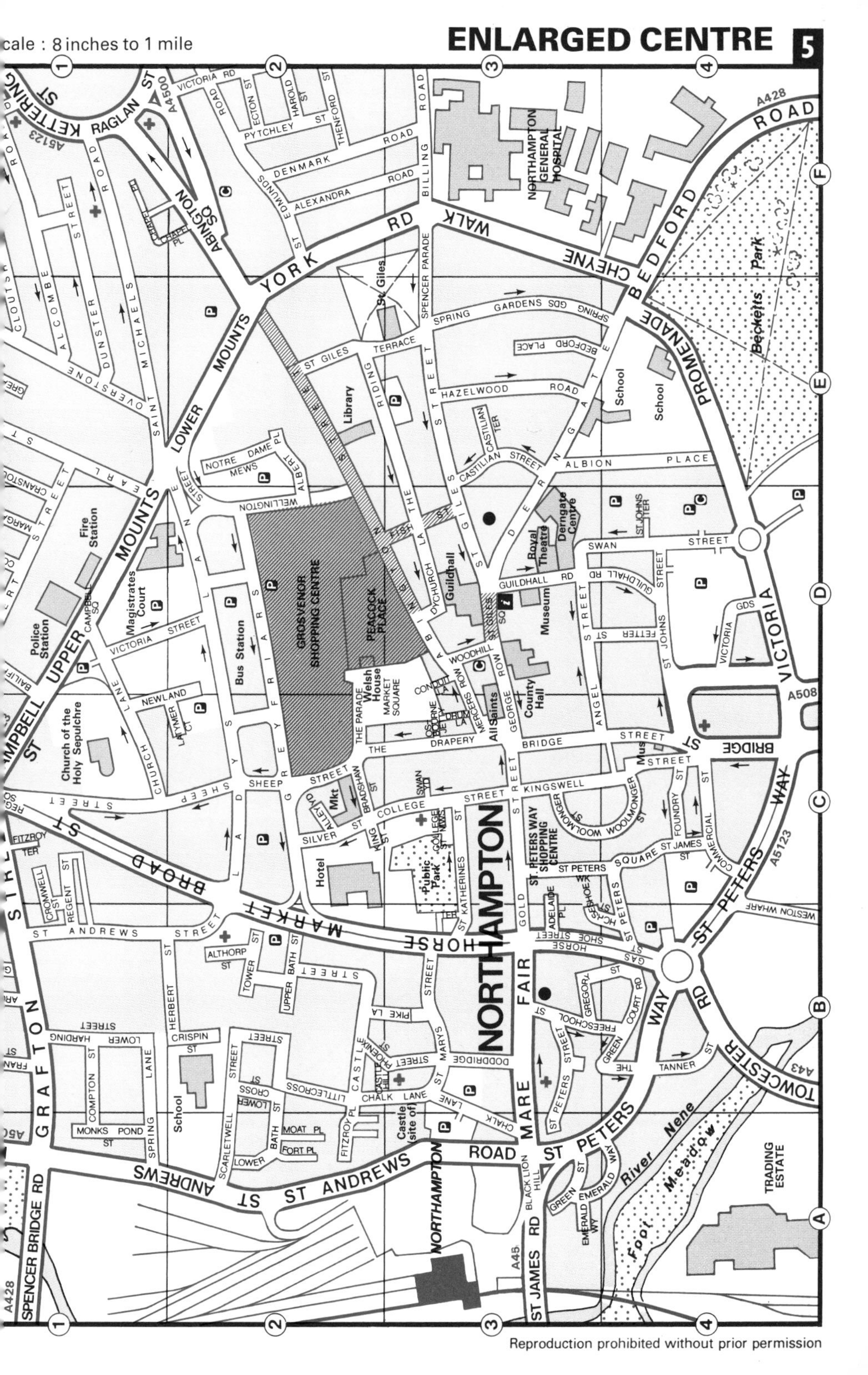
NORTHAMPTON
GROSVENOR SHOPPING CENTRE
PEACOCK PLACE
NORTHAMPTON GENERAL HOSPITAL
Beckets Park
Derngate Centre
Royal Theatre
Guildhall
Museum
County Hall
All Saints
Library
St Giles
Bus Station
Magistrates Court
Fire Station
Police Station
Church of the Holy Sepulchre
Welsh House
MARKET SQUARE
Mkt
Hotel
Public Park
ST PETERS WAY SHOPPING CENTRE
School
Castle (site of)
TRADING ESTATE
River Nene
Foot Meadow
YORK RD
CHEYNE WALK
BEDFORD ROAD
PROMENADE
VICTORIA
MOUNTS
UPPER MOUNTS
LOWER MOUNTS
BROAD ST
HORSE MARKET
MARE FAIR
GOLD ST
ST ANDREWS ROAD
ST PETERS WAY
TOWCESTER RD
GRAFTON ST
SPENCER BRIDGE RD
ST JAMES RD
KETTERING RD
ABINGTON SQ
SHEEP STREET
BRIDGE STREET
THE DRAPERY
ST GILES STREET
DERNGATE
ABINGTON STREET
A428
A4500
A5123
A508
A43
A45

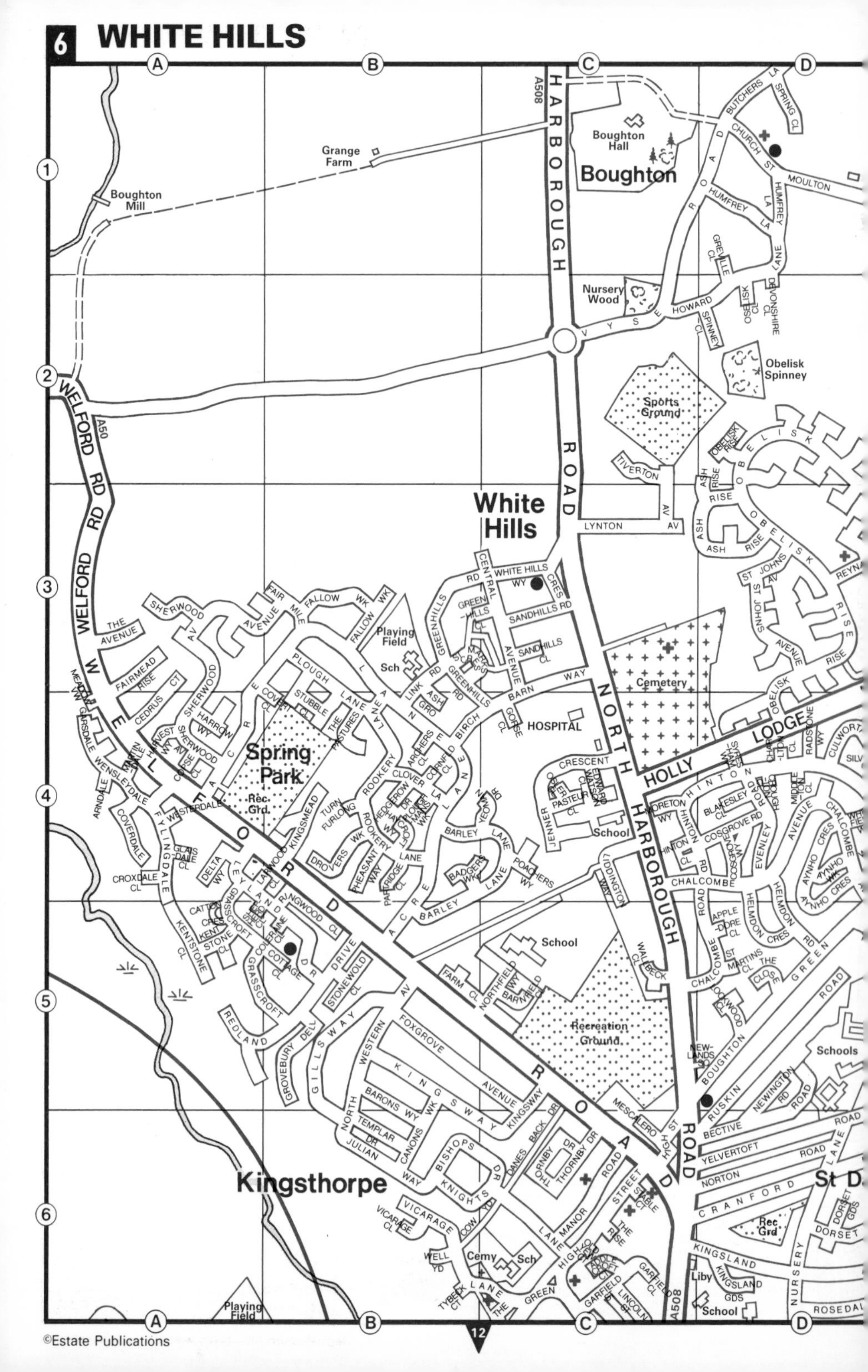

Boughton
Boughton Hall
Grange Farm
Boughton Mill
Nursery Wood
Obelisk Spinney
Sports Ground
White Hills
Playing Field
Sch
Cemetery
HOSPITAL
Spring Park
Rec. Grd.
School
Recreation Ground
Schools
Kingsthorpe
Cemy
Sch
Liby
School
Rec Grd
St D
HARBOROUGH ROAD
NORTH HARBOROUGH ROAD
WELFORD RD
WELFORD ROAD
HOLLY LODGE
KINGSWAY

12

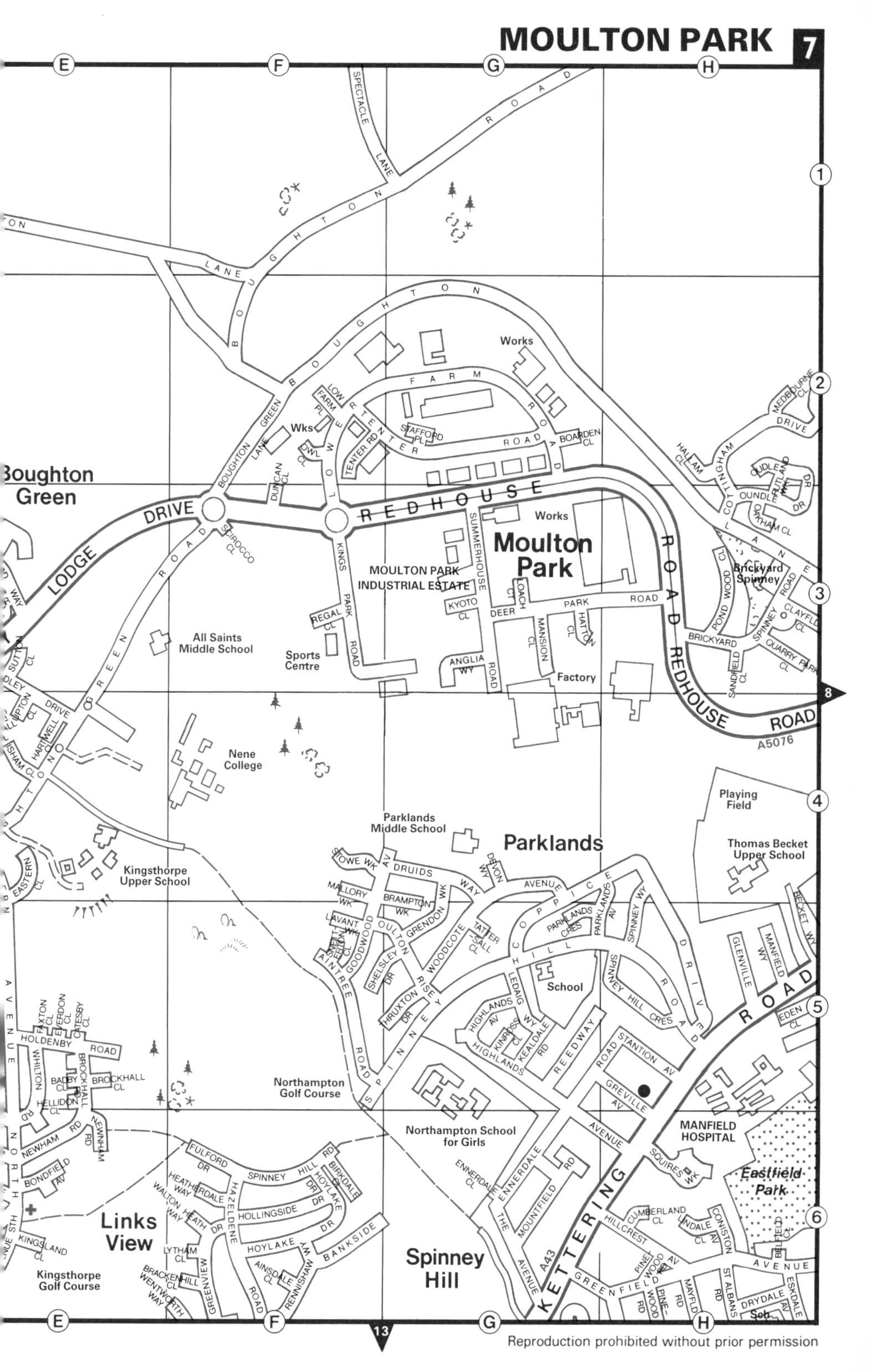
E
F
G
H
1
2
3
4
5
6
8
13
Boughton Green
Moulton Park
MOULTON PARK INDUSTRIAL ESTATE
All Saints Middle School
Sports Centre
Nene College
Works
Wks
Factory
Brickyard Spinney
Playing Field
Thomas Becket Upper School
Parklands Middle School
Parklands
Kingsthorpe Upper School
School
Northampton Golf Course
Northampton School for Girls
MANFIELD HOSPITAL
Eastfield Park
Links View
Spinney Hill
Kingsthorpe Golf Course
BOUGHTON LANE
SPECTACLE LANE
BOUGHTON GREEN LANE
BOUGHTON GREEN ROAD
LODGE DRIVE
REDHOUSE ROAD
FARM ROAD
TENTER ROAD
LOW FARM PL
OWL CL
TENTER RD
STAFFORD PL
BOARDEN CL
DUNCAN CL
SIROCCO CL
KINGS PARK ROAD
REGAL CL
SUMMERHOUSE ROAD
KYOTO CL
ANGLIA WY
DEER PARK ROAD
LOACH CT
MANSION CL
HATTON CL
COTTINGHAM LANE
HALLAM CL
MEDBOURNE CL
DRIVE
OUNDLE DR
RUTLAND WK
OAKHAM CL
POND WOOD CL
SPINNEY ROAD
CLAYFLD CL
BRICKYARD
QUARRY PARK CL
SANDFIELD CL
A5076
SUTTON CL
DRIVE
HARTWELL CL
EASTERN CL
STOWE WK
DRUIDS WAY
MALLORY WK
BRAMPTON WK
GRENDON WK
LAVANT WK
OULTON RISE
GOODWOOD
SHELSLEY DR
AINTREE ROAD
THRUXTON DR
WOODCOTE
TATTERSALL CL
DEVON WY
AVENUE
COPPICE HILL
PARKLANDS CRES
PARKLANDS AV
SPINNEY WY
SPINNEY HILL CRES
SPINNEY HILL ROAD
SPINNEY DRIVE
LEDAIG WY
HIGHLANDS AV
KINROSS CL
KEALDALE RD
HIGHLANDS
REEDWAY
STANTION AV
ROAD
GREVILLE AV
AVENUE
GLENVILLE
MANFIELD WY
BECKET WY
EDEN CL
ROAD
SQUIRES WK
KETTERING
A43
ENNERDALE CL
ENNERDALE RD
MOUNTFIELD RD
THE AVENUE
CUMBERLAND CL
LINDALE CL
CONISTON AV
HILLCREST AV
BELFIELD CL
AVENUE
GREENFIELD RD
PINEWOOD RD
PINE-WOOD RD
MAYFLD RD
ST ALBANS RD
DRYDALE AV
ESKDALE
Sch
FAXTON CL
EVERDON CL
CATESBY CL
HOLDENBY ROAD
WHILTON
BADBY CL
BROCKHALL
BROCKHALL CL
HELLIDON CL
NEWHAM RD
NEWHAM
BONDFIELD AV
KINGSLAND CL
AVENUE
NORTH
FULFORD DR
SPINNEY HILL RD
BIRKDALE CL
HOYLAKE DR
HEATHERDALE WAY
WALTON HEATH WAY
HAZELDENE
HOLLINGSIDE DR
HOYLAKE WAY
BANKSIDE
LYTHAM CL
AINSDALE CL
RENNISHAW WAY
BRACKENHILL
WENTWORTH WAY
GREENVIEW
ROAD

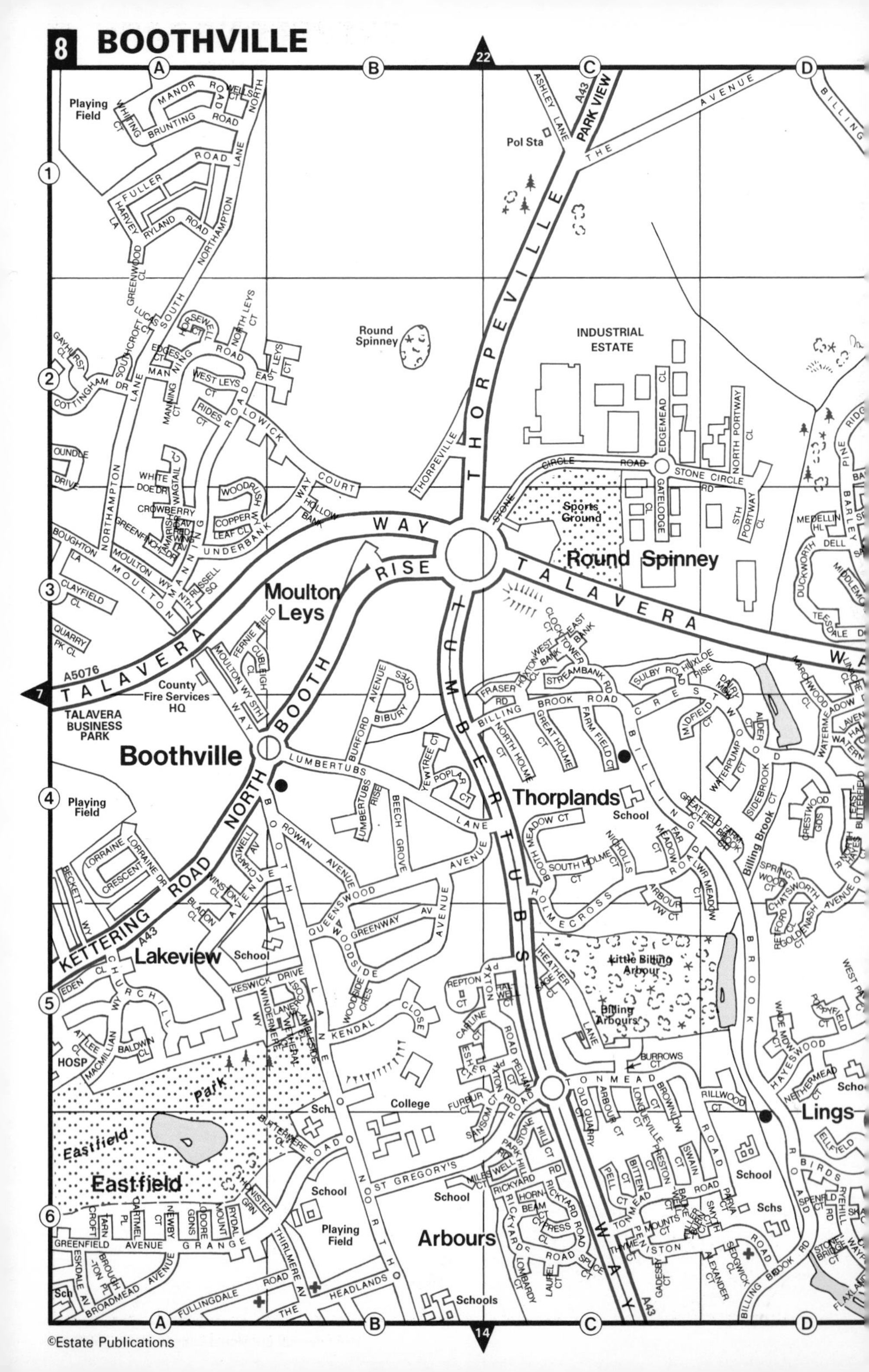
8
BOOTHVILLE
A
B
C
D
1
2
3
4
5
6
22
14
7
Playing Field
MANOR ROAD
WELLS CT
BRUNTING ROAD
FULLER
HARVEY LA
RYLAND ROAD
GREENWOOD CL
NORTHAMPTON LANE NORTH
NORTHAMPTON LANE SOUTH
SOUTHCROFT
LUCAS CT
GAYHURST
COTTINGHAM DR
HORSEWELL CT
NORTH LEYS CT
EDGES CT
MANNING ROAD
WEST LEYS CT
EAST LEYS CT
MANNING CT
RIDES CT
LOWICK
OUNDLE DRIVE
WHITE DOE DR
WAGTAIL CT
WOODRUSH WAY
CROWBERRY
COPPER LEAF CL
UNDERBANK
HOLLOW BANK
WAY COURT
GREENFINCH DR
BOUGHTON LA
MOULTON WY NTH
RUSSELL SQ
CLAYFIELD CL
QUARRY PK CL
TALAVERA WAY
A5076
Round Spinney
THORPEVILLE
ASHLEY LANE
A43
PARK VIEW
THE AVENUE
Pol Sta
INDUSTRIAL ESTATE
EDGEMEAD CL
NORTH PORTWAY CL
CIRCLE ROAD
STONE CIRCLE RD
GATELODGE CL
STH PORTWAY CL
STONE
Sports Ground
Round Spinney
Moulton Leys
RISE
BOOTH
FERNIE FIELD
CUBLEIGH
MOULTON WY STH
WAY
County Fire Services HQ
TALAVERA BUSINESS PARK
Boothville
LUMBERTUBS
BURFORD AVENUE
BIBURY CRES
YEWTREE CT
POPLAR CT
LUMBERTUBS RISE
BEECH GROVE
LANE
CLOCKTOWER CT
EAST BANK
WEST BANK
HOXTON CL
STREAMBANK RD
FRASER RD
BILLING BROOK ROAD
NORTH HOLME CT
GREAT HOLME CT
FARM FIELD CT
SULBY ROAD
HUXLOE RISE
DAIRY MDW
CRESTWOOD
MIDFIELD CT
WATERPLUMP CT
ALDER
SIDEBROOK CT
Thorplands
School
BOOTH MEADOW CT
NICHOLLS CT
SOUTH HOLME CT
HOLMECROSS
GREAT FIELD
FAR MEADOW CT
FARM BROOK
LWR MEADOW CT
ARBOUR VW CT
Billing Brook
MEDELLIN HL
DUCKWORTH DELL
BARLEY
MIDDLEMO
TEESDALE
PINE RIDGE
MARCHWOOD CL
WATERMEADOW
CRESTWOOD GDS
SPRINGWOOD CT
CHATSWORTH AVENUE
RETFORD CT
GOLDENASH CT
Playing Field
LORRAINE CRESCENT
LORRAINE DR
BECKETT WY
KETTERING ROAD NORTH
CHARWELL AV
WINSTON CL
BLADON CL
AVENUE
ROWAN AVENUE
QUEENSWOOD
GREENWAY AV
AVENUE
WOODSIDE
WOODSIDE CRES
Lakeview
School
CHURCHILL
EDEN CL
KESWICK DRIVE
WINDERMERE WY
LANERCOST
AMBLESIDE
WETHERAL
KENDAL
CLOSE
ATTLEE
MACMILLIAN
BALDWIN CL
HOSP
Park
College
Sch
BUTTERMERE CL
Eastfield
Eastfield
REPTON CT
PAXTON
HALLWELL CT
CARLINE CT
ESHER CT
PAXTON RD
PELHAM ROAD
FURBUR CT
SANSOM CT
HEATHER
SAGE CL
Little Billing Arbour
Billing Arbours
BURROWS CT
TONMEAD
OLD QUARRY CT
ARBOUR CT
LONGUEVILLE CT
BROWNLOW CT
RILLWOOD CT
Lings
ST GREGORY'S ROAD
School
MILESWELL CT
PARK HILL CT
STONE HILL CT
RICKYARD RD
HORNBEAM CL
CYPRESS CL
RICKYARD ROAD
LOMBARDY CT
LAUREL CT
SPRUCE
PELL CT
BITTEN CT
PRESTON CT
SWAIN CT
SMYTH CT
PARVA CT
THYME CT
PENISTON
MOUNTS CT
GADESBY CT
ALEXANDER CT
SEDGWICK CL
School
Schs
Arbours
Playing Field
School
Schools
NORTH
HEADLANDS
THE
THIRLMERE AV
FULLINGDALE ROAD
DUNSTER GRN
GREENFIELD AVENUE
GRANGE
CROFT
TARN CT
CARTMEL PL
NEWBY CT
GDNS
ODORE
MOUNT
RYDAL
BROUGHTON PL
ESKDALE AV
BROADMEAD AVENUE
Sch
WEST PAD
POPPYFIELD
WADE MDW
HAYESWOOD
NETHERMEAD
Scho
ELLFIELD
BIRDS
SPENFIELD CT
RYEHILL
STONE BRIDGE
FLAXLAND
BILLING BROOK RD
ROAD
WAY
A43
©Estate Publications

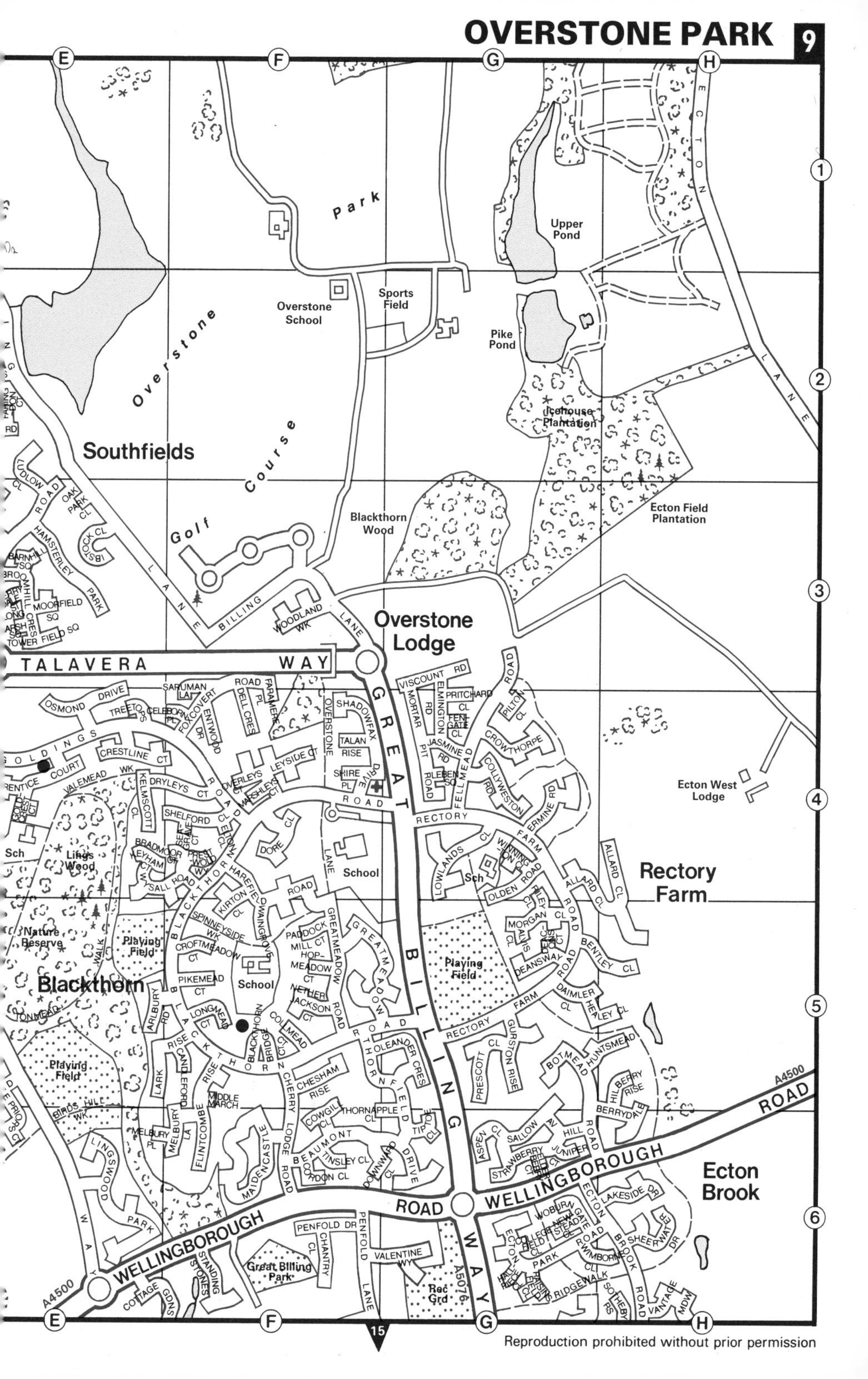
Overstone Park
Overstone Golf Course
Overstone School
Sports Field
Upper Pond
Pike Pond
Icehouse Plantation
Ecton Field Plantation
Blackthorn Wood
Southfields
Overstone Lodge
Ecton West Lodge
Rectory Farm
Blackthorn
Lings Wood
Nature Reserve
Playing Field
School
Ecton Brook
Great Billing Park
Rec Grd
TALAVERA WAY
GREAT BILLING WAY
WELLINGBOROUGH ROAD
A4500
A5076
ECTON LANE
BILLING LANE
OVERSTONE LANE

15

New Duston
HARLESTONE
A428
Slatepit Plantation
Fleetland Farm
Bottomclose Spinney
Heath Farm
Roman Road
Errington Park
School
Playing Field
ST. CRISPIN HOSPITAL
Berry Wood
Cricket Ground
Norwood Farm
Cemy
PRINCESS
HOSPI
LARKHALL LANE
SANDY LANE
BERRYWOOD ROAD
PORT ROAD
MAIN ROAD
WEGGS FARM ROAD
RYLAND ROAD
LARCH LA
WOODLEY CHASE
DEANCOURT DR
PARK LA
RAWLEY CRES
EATON ROAD

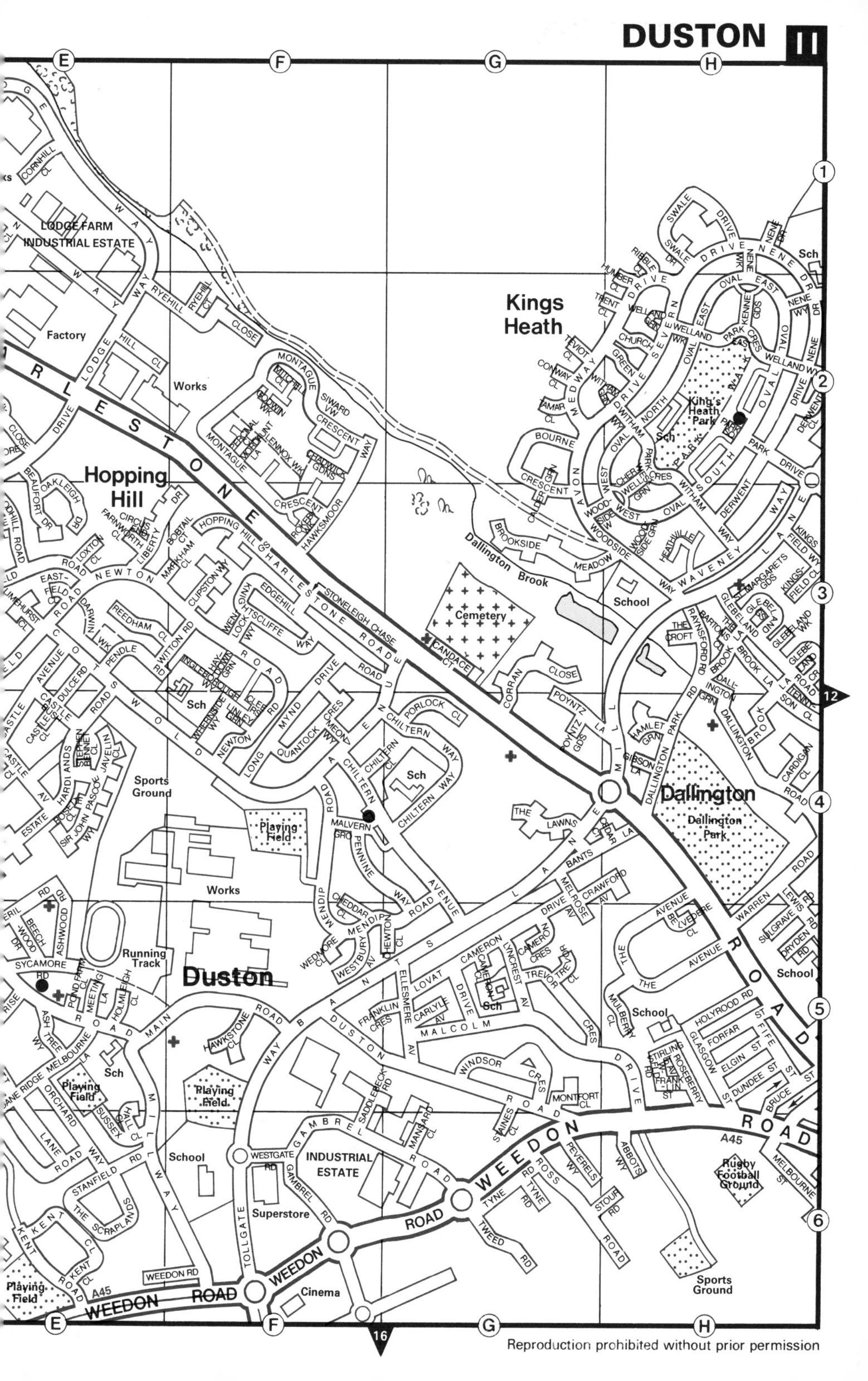
E
F
G
H
1
2
3
4
5
6
12
16
LODGE FARM INDUSTRIAL ESTATE
Factory
Works
CORNHILL CL
LODGE WAY
RYEHILL CL
RYEHILL CLOSE
HILL CL
LODGE DRIVE
HARLESTONE ROAD
Hopping Hill
MONTAGUE CRESCENT
MITCHELL CL
GODWIN WK
PERCIVAL CL
MORDAUNT LA
LENNOX WK
SIWARD VW
CHADWICK GDNS
ROKEBY WK
HAWKSMOOR WAY
Kings Heath
SWALE DRIVE
SWALE DR
NENE DR
NENE DRIVE
NENE WY
Sch
RIBBLE CL
HUMBER CL
TRENT CL
WELLAND GRN
WELLAND WK
WELLAND WY
CHURCH GREEN
SEVERN DRIVE
TEVIOT CL
CONWAY CL
TAMAR CL
MEDWAY DRIVE
WITHAM WY
OVAL EAST
EAST OVAL
KENNET GDNS
PARK CRES EAST
King's Heath Park
PARK RD
PARK WALK SOUTH
OVAL NORTH
WEST OVAL
BOURNE CRESCENT
CALDER GRN
AVON DRIVE
CHERWELL GRN
PARK CRES
WITHAM WAY
DERWENT WAY
DERWENT CL
PARK DRIVE
WAVENEY WAY
WOODSIDE WY
WOODSIDE GRN
HEATHVILLE
KINGS FIELD WY
KINGSFIELD CL
ST MARGARETS GDNS
BROOKSIDE MEADOW
Dallington Brook
School
Cemetery
CANDACE CT
CORRAN CLOSE
POYNTZ LA
POYNTZ GDNS
MILL LANE
THE CROFT
RAYNSFORD RD
BARTONS CL
GLEBELAND RD
GLEBELAND WK
GLEBE LAND CT
BROOK LA
DALLINGTON GRN
DALLINGTON BROOK
TENNYSON CL
CARDIGAN CL
HAMLET GRN
GIBSON LA
DALLINGTON PARK RD
Dallington
Dallington Park
BEAUFORT DR
OAKLEIGH DR
CIRCUS END
FARNWORTH CL
LIBERTY DR
BOBTAIL CT
HOPPING HILL GDNS
MARKHAM CL
CLIPSTON WY
KINGSTHORPE
EDGEHILL WAY
WENLOCK WY
HITCHCLIFFE WY
STONELEIGH CHASE
LOXTON CL
EASTFIELD CL
NEWTON ROAD
DARWIN WK
REEDHAM CL
PENDLE RD
WITTON RD
HAYDOWN GRN
INGLEBOROUGH GRN
KINGS ROAD
CLEE RISE
LINLEY GRN
WHERNSIDE WY
NEWTON RD
LONG MYND DRIVE
QUANTOCK CRES
MEON WY
CHILTERN AVENUE
CHILTERN CL
PORLOCK CL
CHILTERN WAY
ASHFORD ROAD
ROAD
AVENUE
DULCE RD
CASTLE CL
CASTLE AV
STEPHEN BENNETT CL
JAVELIN CL
HARDLANDS
FOSTER CL
SIR JOHN PASCOE WY
ESTATE AV
WOLD ROAD
Sports Ground
Playing Field
MALVERN GRO
PENNINE WAY
THE LAWNS
CEDAR LA
BANTS LANE
Works
MENDIP RD
CHEDDAR CL
MENDIP
CHEWTON CL
WEDMORE
WESTBURY AV
MELROSE AV
CRAWFORD AV
BELVEDERE CL
THE AVENUE
WARREN ROAD
LEWIS RD
SULGRAVE
DRYDEN RD
School
BEECHWOOD DR
ASHWOOD RD
SYCAMORE RD
Running Track
Duston
POND FARM CL
MEETING LA
HOLMLEIGH CL
ASH TREE WY
MELBOURNE LA
MAIN ROAD
HAWKSTONE CL
ELLESMERE AV
LOVAT
FRANKLIN CRES
CARLYLE AV
CAMERON DRIVE
CAMERON CRES
LYNCREST AV
TREVOR CL
TREVOR CRES
MALCOLM
DUSTON ROAD
MULBERRY CL
HOLYROOD RD
FORFAR ST
FIFE ST
ELGIN ST
DUNDEE ST
GLASGOW ST
ROSEBERY ST
STIRLING RD
FRANKLIN ST
BRUCE ST
Sch
Playing Field
SUSSEX CL
HALL CL
ORCHARD LANE
ROAD WAY
STANFIELD RD
MILL WAY
School
WINDSOR CRES
MONTFORT CL
SAXONS CL
SADDLEBECK RD
MANSARD CL
GAMBREL ROAD
WESTGATE RD
INDUSTRIAL ESTATE
GAMBREL RD
Superstore
TOLLGATE
PEVERELS WY
ABBOTS WY
A45
WEEDON ROAD
ROSS RD
TYNE RD
TWEED RD
STOUR RD
Rugby Football Ground
MELBOURNE ST
KENT ROAD
KENT CL
THE SCRAPLANDS
Playing Field
WEEDON RD
Cinema
Sports Ground

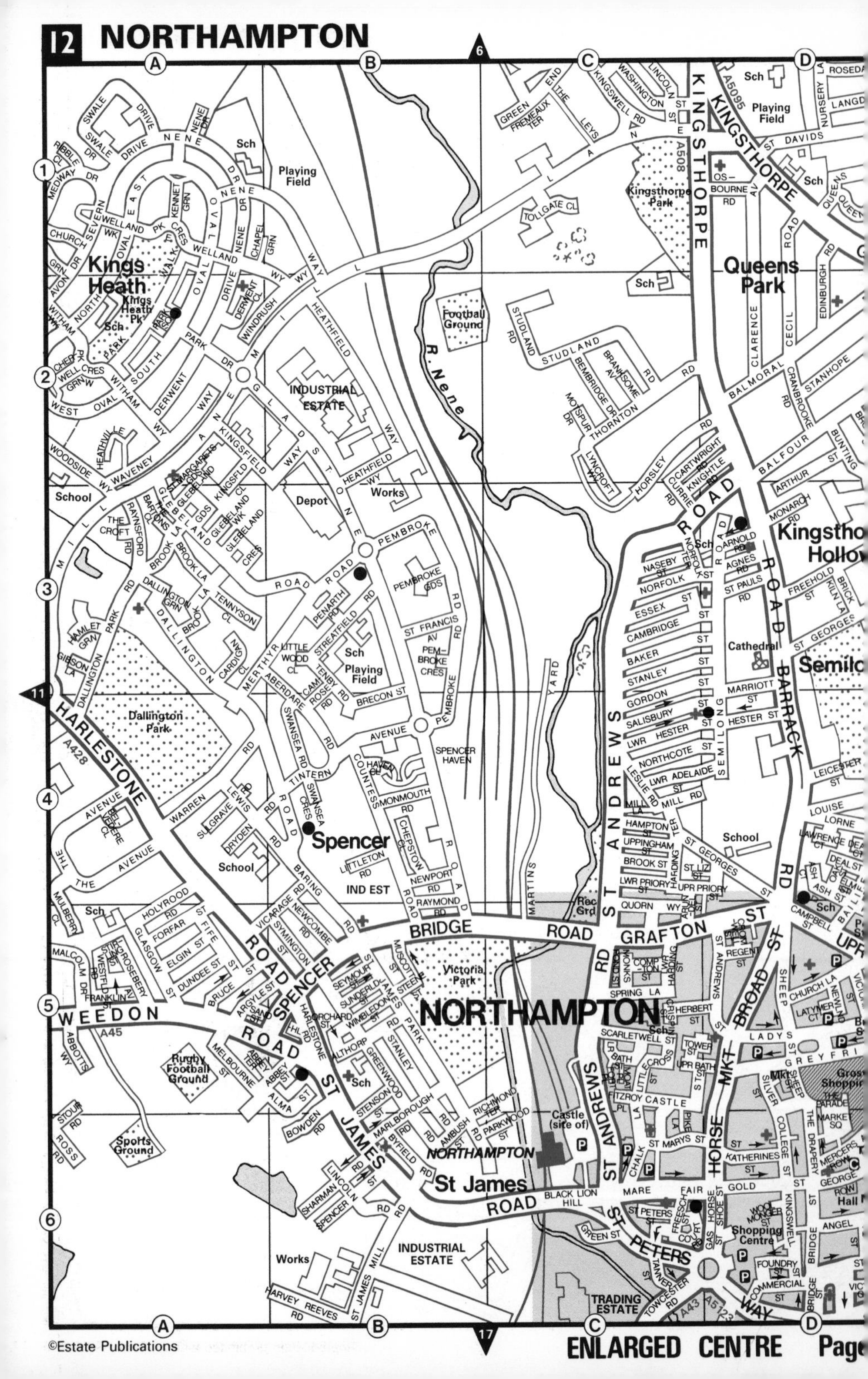
12
NORTHAMPTON
A
B
C
D
6
1
2
3
4
5
6
11
17
Kings Heath
Kings Heath Pk
Playing Field
Sch
School
Industrial Estate
Depot
Works
Football Ground
R. Nene
Kingsthorpe Park
Queens Park
Kingsthorpe
Cathedral
Dallington Park
Spencer
IND EST
Spencer Haven
Victoria Park
NORTHAMPTON
Rugby Football Ground
Sports Ground
St James
Castle (site of)
Shopping Centre
Trading Estate
Rec Grd
HARLESTONE
A428
WEEDON ROAD
A45
SPENCER ROAD
BRIDGE ROAD
ST JAMES ROAD
ST ANDREWS RD
GRAFTON ST
BARRACK RD
KINGSTHORPE RD
A508
A5095
MILL LANE
GLADSTONE RD
HEATHFIELD WAY
PEMBROKE RD
COUNTESS ROAD
ST JAMES PARK RD
ST JAMES MILL RD
HARVEY REEVES RD
ST PETERS WAY
HORSE MKT
BROAD ST
SHEEP ST
BLACK LION HILL
MARE FAIR
GOLD ST
TOWCESTER RD
A43
A5123
TANNER ST
MARTINS YARD
©Estate Publications
ENLARGED CENTRE Page

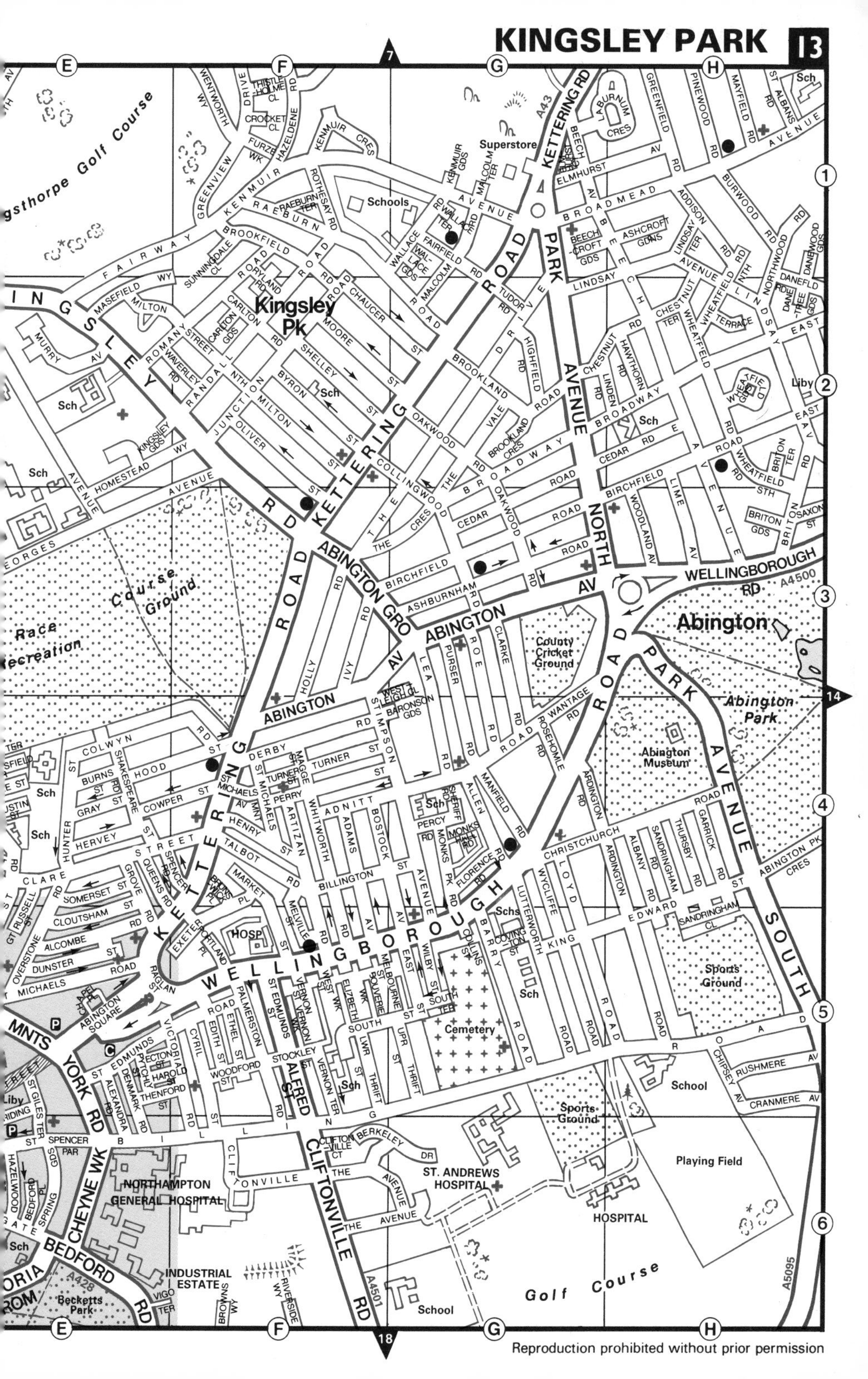
Kingsley Pk
Kingsthorpe Golf Course
Race Course Recreation Ground
Abington
Abington Park
Abington Museum
County Cricket Ground
Sports Ground
Cemetery
School
Playing Field
Golf Course
ST. ANDREWS HOSPITAL
HOSPITAL
NORTHAMPTON GENERAL HOSPITAL
INDUSTRIAL ESTATE
Becketts Park
Superstore
Schools
Liby
HOSP
KETTERING RD
KETTERING ROAD
ABINGTON AV
ABINGTON GRO
WELLINGBOROUGH RD
WELLINGBOROUGH ROAD
PARK AVENUE NORTH
PARK AVENUE SOUTH
KINGSLEY RD
KINGSLEY PARK TER
BROADMEAD AVENUE
BEECH AV
BROADWAY
BROADWAY EAST
CEDAR RD
BIRCHFIELD RD
LINDSAY AV
CHESTNUT RD
WHEATFIELD RD
BILLING ROAD
CLIFTONVILLE RD
CLIFTONVILLE
THE AVENUE
BEDFORD RD
YORK RD
CHEYNE WK
ST GILES TER
SPENCER PAR
ABINGTON SQUARE
FAIRWAY
KENMUIR AVENUE
GREENVIEW
HAZELDENE RD
BROOKFIELD RD
RAEBURN RD
MALCOLM RD
CHAUCER ST
MOORE ST
SHELLEY ST
BYRON ST
MILTON ST
OLIVER ST
JUNCTION RD
ROMANY RD
HOMESTEAD WY
COLLINGWOOD RD
THE CRES
BROOKLAND RD
HIGHFIELD RD
STIMPSON AV
PURSER RD
ROE RD
CLARKE RD
LEA RD
HOLLY RD
IVY RD
ASHBURNHAM RD
WANTAGE RD
ROSEHOLME RD
MANFIELD RD
CHRISTCHURCH RD
ARDINGTON RD
ALBANY RD
SANDRINGHAM RD
THURSBY RD
GARRICK RD
EDWARD RD
KING ST
LUTTERWORTH RD
WYCLIFFE RD
LOYD RD
BARRY RD
COLLINS ST
MELBOURNE ST
EAST ST
WILBY ST
SOUTH ST
ADNITT RD
ADAMS AV
BOSTOCK AV
WHITWORTH RD
ARTIZAN RD
BILLINGTON ST
MELVILLE ST
MARKET ST
TALBOT RD
HENRY ST
COWPER ST
HOOD ST
DERBY RD
TURNER ST
COLWYN RD
SHAKESPEARE RD
HUNTER ST
HERVEY ST
GRAY ST
BURNS ST
CLARE ST
SOMERSET ST
CLOUTSHAM ST
ALCOMBE RD
DUNSTER ST
OVERSTONE RD
ST MICHAELS RD
EXETER PL
PORTLAND PL
RAGLAN ST
PALMERSTON RD
ST EDMUNDS ST
VERNON TER
ALFRED ST
STOCKLEY ST
THRIFT ST
VICTORIA
CYRIL ST
EDITH ST
ETHEL ST
HAROLD ST
WOODFORD ST
THENFORD ST
DENMARK RD
ALEXANDRA RD
HAZELWOOD RD
BERKELEY DR
RUSHMERE AV
CRANMERE AV
CHIPSEY AV
BURWOOD RD
MAYFIELD RD
PINEWOOD RD
GREENFIELD RD
LABURNUM CRES
ELMHURST AV
A43
A4500
A4501
A428
A5095
E
F
G
H
1
2
3
4
5
6
7
14
18

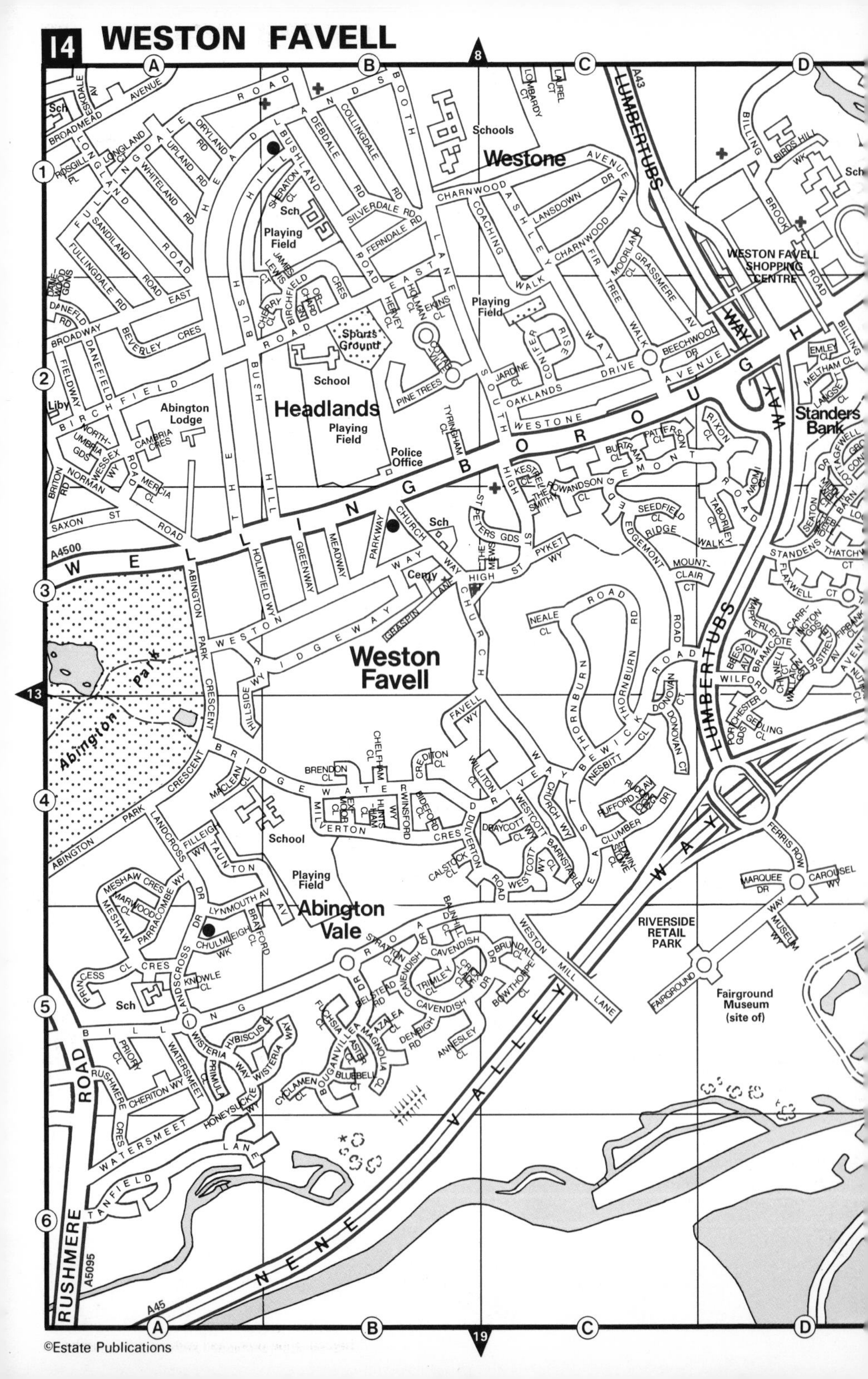
14
WESTON FAVELL
Westone
Schools
WESTON FAVELL SHOPPING CENTRE
Standers Bank
Headlands
Abington Lodge
School
Playing Field
Sports Ground
Police Office
Sch
Liby
Cemy
Weston Favell
Abington Park
Abington Vale
RIVERSIDE RETAIL PARK
Fairground Museum (site of)
WELLINGBOROUGH ROAD
A4500
LUMBERTUBS WAY
A43
NENE VALLEY WAY
A45
RUSHMERE ROAD
A5095
ABINGTON PARK CRESCENT
BRIDGEWATER DRIVE
WESTON WAY
RIDGEWAY
CHURCH WAY
HIGH ST
BILLING ROAD
BILLING BROOK ROAD
WESTON MILL LANE
BIRCHFIELD ROAD EAST
HEADLANDS
THE BUSH HILL
BOOTH LANE SOUTH
CHARNWOOD AVENUE
BEECHWOOD DRIVE
EDGEMONT ROAD
THORNBURN ROAD
BEWICK ROAD
FULLINGDALE ROAD
BROADMEAD AVENUE
LANDCROSS DR
BILLING LANE
WATERSMEET
STRATON DR
CAVENDISH DR
MARQUEE DR
CAROUSEL WY
FERRIS ROW
FAIRGROUND WY
MUSEUM WY
©Estate Publications

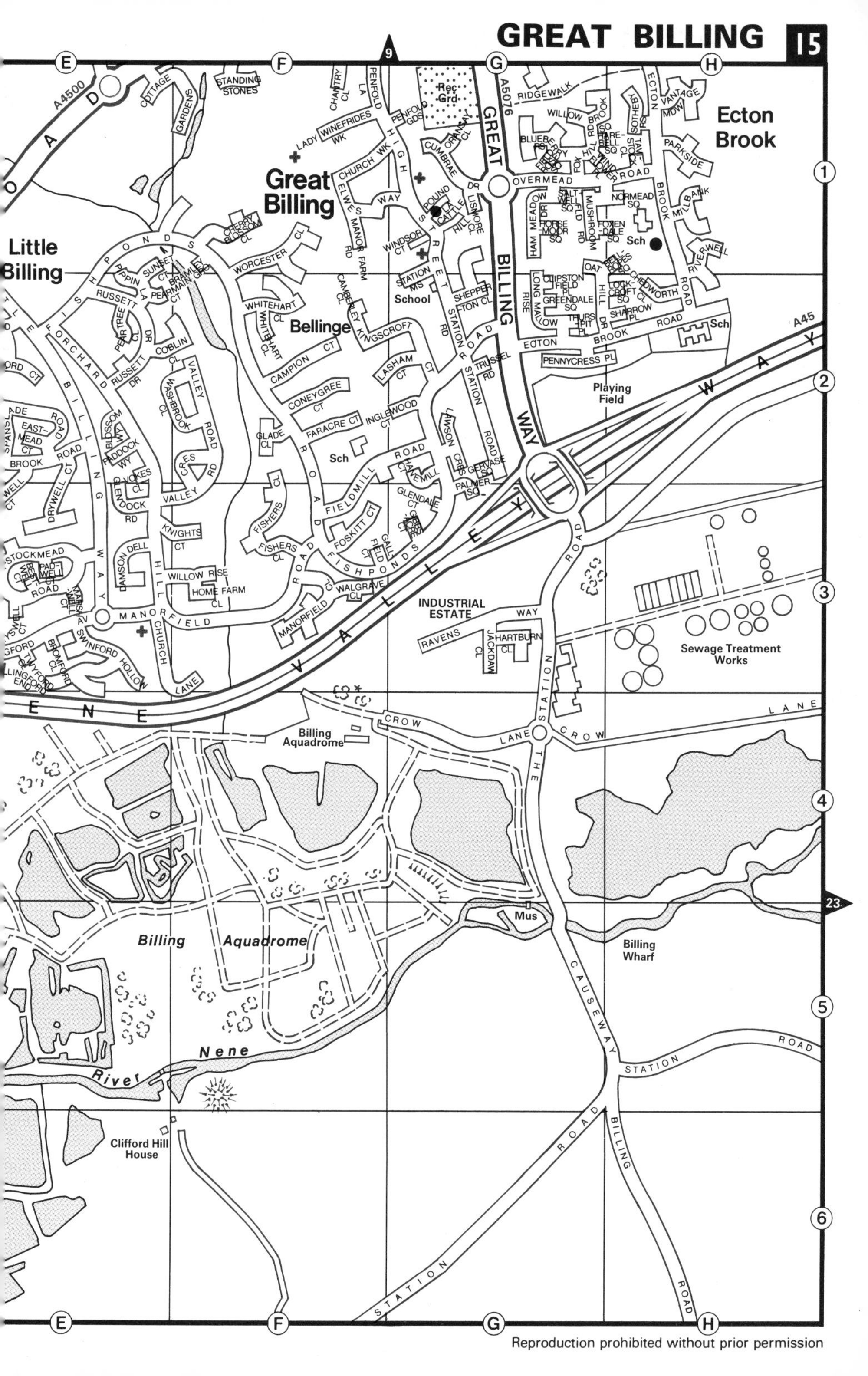
Great Billing
Little Billing
Ecton Brook
Bellinge
School
Sch
Rec Grd
Playing Field
INDUSTRIAL ESTATE
Sewage Treatment Works
Billing Aquadrome
Billing Wharf
Mus
Clifford Hill House
River Nene
A4500
A5076
A45
GREAT BILLING WAY
NENE VALLEY WAY
FISHPONDS ROAD
BILLING WAY
CHURCH LANE
CROW LANE
THE CAUSEWAY
STATION ROAD
BILLING ROAD
ECTON BROOK ROAD
OVERMEAD
HIGH STREET
MANORFIELD
VALLEY ROAD
23
9

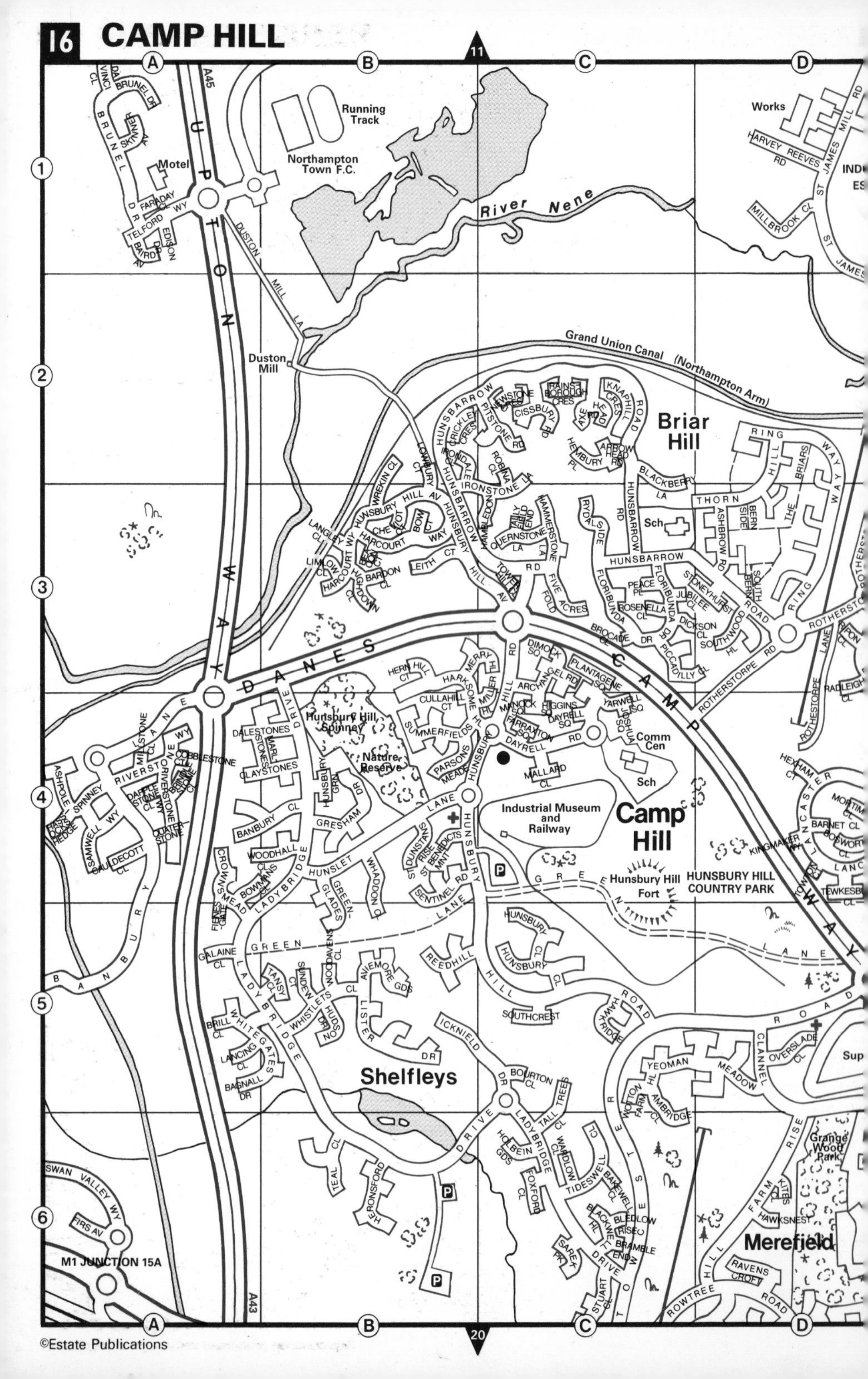

A
B
C
D
11
1
2
3
4
5
6
20
Running Track
Northampton Town F.C.
Motel
Works
River Nene
Grand Union Canal (Northampton Arm)
Duston Mill
UPTON WAY
DANES CAMP WAY
A45
A43
DUSTON MILL LA
BRUNEL DR
BRUNEL CL
DALVINCI CL
JENNY SKINNER AV
FARADAY CL
TELFORD WY
BAIRD AV
EDISON DR
HARVEY REEVES RD
ST JAMES MILL RD
MILLBROOK CL
Briar Hill
HUNSBARROW RD
KNAPHILL CRES
RAINSBOROUGH CRES
CISSBURY RD
AXE HEAD RD
ARROW HEAD RD
HEMBURY PL
PITSTONE RD
ROBINA CL
IRONSTONE LA
BLACKBERRY LA
RING WAY
THE BRIARS
THORN HILL
ASHBROW RD
BERN SIDE
SOUTH BERN
Sch
RYDAL SIDE
HAMMERSTONE LA
QUERNSTONE LA
FIVE ACRES
FOLD
TOWER HILL
FLORIBUNDA DR
PEACE PL
ROSENELLA CL
JUBILEE CL
STONEYHURST
DICKSON CL
SOUTHWOOD HL
BROCADE DR
PICCADILLY CL
ROTHERSTORPE RD
ROTHERSTORPE LANE
RADLEIGH CL
LOWBURY CT
WREKIN CL
HUNSBURY HILL AV
HUNSBURY HILL RD
CHEVIOT CL
BOW CT
WAY
HARCOURT WY
LANGLEY WY
LANGLEY CL
LIMLOW CL
HIGHDOWN CL
BARDON CL
LEITH CT
HAMBLEDON CL
HERN HILL CT
HARKSOME HL
MERRY HL
MILLER HL
CULLAHILL CT
SUMMERFIELDS
PARSONS MEADE
DIMOCK SQ
ARCHANGEL RD
PLANTAGENET SQ
YARWELL SQ
JOSHUA SQ
HIGGINS SQ
DAYRELL SQ
DAYRELL RD
FARRAXTON SQ
MANOCK SQ
MALLARD CL
Comm Cen
Hunsbury Hill Spinney
Nature Reserve
Industrial Museum and Railway
Camp Hill
Hunsbury Hill Fort
HUNSBURY HILL COUNTRY PARK
GREEN LANE
KINGMAKER WY
LANCASTER WAY
HEXHAM CT
BARNET CL
BOSWORTH CL
TEWKESBURY CL
TOWTON CL
MILLSTONE CL
RIVERSTONE WY
COBBLESTONE
ASHPOLE SPINNEY
SAMWELL WY
CAULDECOTT CL
BANBURY LANE
DALESTONES
CLAYSTONES
BANBURY CL
WOODHALL
CROWNSMEAD
BOWMANS
LADYBRIDGE DRIVE
HUNSLET LANE
GRESHAM DR
HUNSBURY GRN
GLADES
GREEN-WHADDON CL
ST DUNSTANS RISE
ST BENEDICTS MNT
SENTINEL RD
HUNSBURY HILL
FIENES GATE
GALAINE CL
TANSY CL
SUNDEW CT
WOODAVENS CL
AVIEMORE GDS
WHISTLETS CL
HUDSONS
REEDHILL
LISTER DR
ICKNIELD DR
HUNSBURY CL
HUNSBURY HILL ROAD
HAWKRIDGE
SOUTHCREST
BRILL CL
WHITEGATES
LANCING CL
BAGNALL DR
Shelfleys
BOURTON CL
TALL TREES
HOLBEIN GDS
FOXFORD CL
WARDLOW CL
TIDESWELL CL
BAKEWELL CL
BLACKWELL HL
BLEDLOW RISE
BRAMBLE END
SAREK PK
STUART CL
TOWCESTER DRIVE
TEAL CL
HERONSFORD
YEOMAN
WOTTON FARM HL
AMBRIDGE
MEADOW
CLANNELL ROAD
OVERSLADE CL
Sup
Grange Wood Park
FARM HILL RISE
KITES CL
HAWKSNEST
Merefield
RAVENS CROFT
ROWTREE ROAD
SWAN VALLEY WY
FIRS AV
M1 JUNCTION 15A

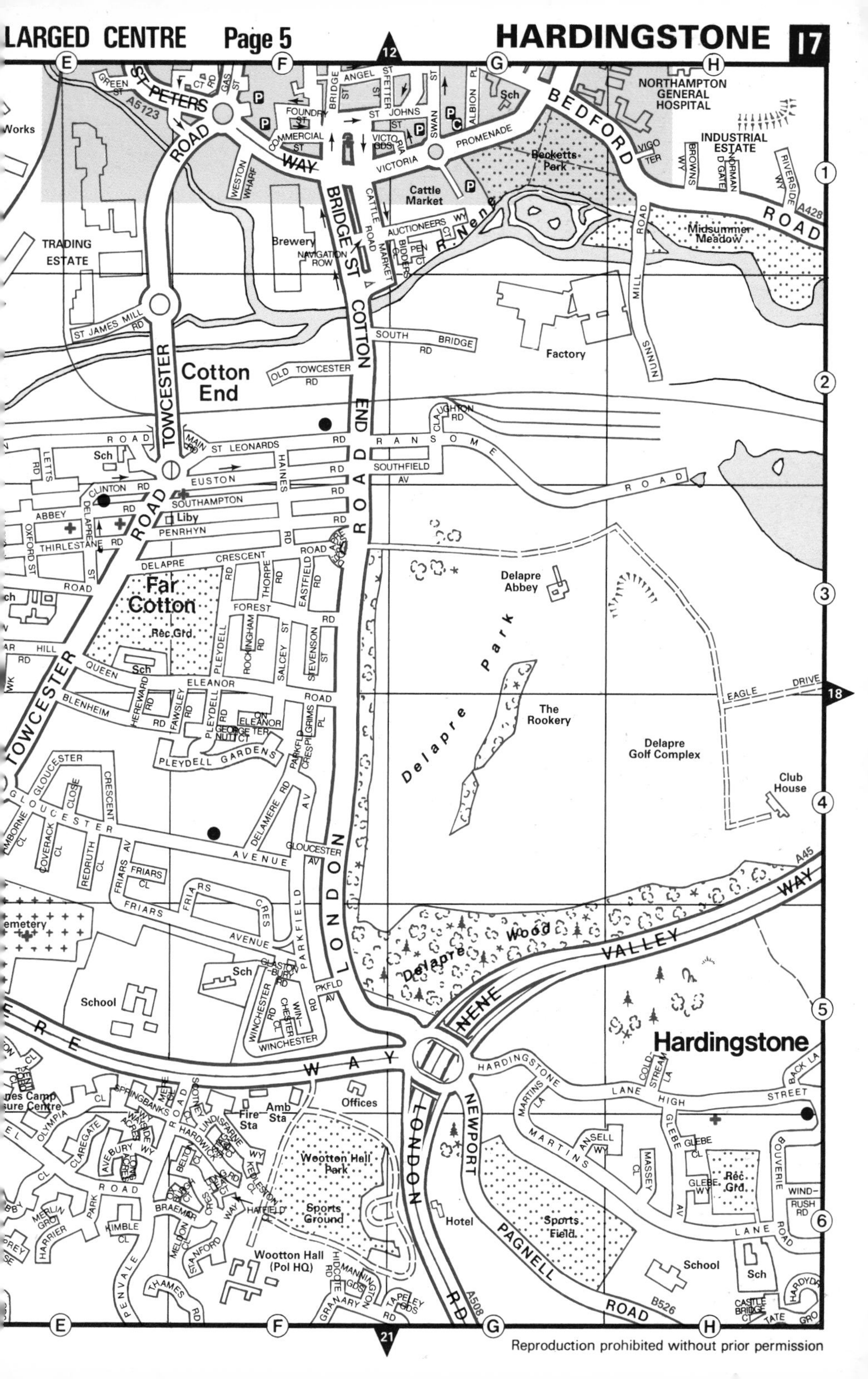
Works
TRADING ESTATE
ST PETERS
ROAD
GREEN ST
A5723
GAS ST
CT RD
FOUNDRY ST
COMMERCIAL ST
WAY
BRIDGE ST
ANGEL ST
FETTER ST
ST JOHNS ST
VICTORIA GDS
SWAN ST
ALBION PL
Sch
PROMENADE
VICTORIA
BEDFORD
NORTHAMPTON GENERAL HOSPITAL
INDUSTRIAL ESTATE
VIGO TER
BROWNS WY
D'GATE
NORMAN
RIVERSIDE WY
A428
ROAD
Beckets Park
Cattle Market
WESTON WHARF
Brewery
NAVIGATION ROW
CATTLE ROAD
AUCTIONEERS WY
MARKET
BIDDERS
PEN CT
R. Nene
MILL ROAD
Midsummer Meadow
Factory
NUNNS
ST JAMES MILL RD
SOUTH BRIDGE RD
OLD TOWCESTER RD
Cotton End
TOWCESTER
COTTON END
ROAD
CLAUGHTON RD
RANSOME
ROAD
MAIN
ST LEONARDS RD
LETTS RD
Sch
EUSTON
HAINES
SOUTHFIELD AV
CLINTON RD
SOUTHAMPTON
ABBEY
DELAPRE
Liby
PENRHYN
OXFORD ST
THIRLESTANE RD
DELAPRE CRESCENT
ROAD
Far Cotton
Rec.Grd.
THORPE RD
EASTFIELD RD
FOREST RD
PLEYDELL
ROCKINGHAM RD
SALCEY ST
STEVENSON ST
Delapre Abbey
Delapre Park
The Rookery
EAGLE DRIVE
Delapre Golf Complex
Club House
HILL RD
QUEEN
Sch
ELEANOR ROAD
HEREWARD RD
FAWSLEY
BLENHEIM RD
ELEANOR TER
GEORGE NUTT CT
CRESPIN
GRIMS PL
PARKFIELD
PLEYDELL GARDENS
GLOUCESTER CRESCENT
CLOSE
DELAMERE RD
AV
GLOUCESTER AV
GLOUCESTER AVENUE
CAMBORNE CL
COVERACK CL
REDRUTH CL
FRIARS AV
FRIARS CL
FRIARS CRES
FRIARS AVENUE
PARKFIELD
LONDON
Cemetery
School
Sch
GLASTONBURY RD
WINCHESTER CL
WIN-CHESTER CL
WINCHESTER
PKFLD AV
A45
WAY
VALLEY
NENE
Delapre Wood
Hardingstone
HARDINGSTONE LANE
COLD STREAM LA
BACK LA
HIGH STREET
WAY
MARTINS LA
MARTINS
ANSELL WY
MASSEY CL
GLEBE AV
GLEBE CL
GLEBE WY
Rec. Grd.
BOUVERIE RD
WIND-RUSH RD
LANE ROAD
Offices
Amb Sta
Fire Sta
SPRINGBANKS WY
CLAREGATE
OLYMPIA
WAYSIDE ACRES
AVEBURY WY
HARDWICK
LINDISFARNE WY
KEDLESTON WAY
HATFIELD
ROAD
Wootton Hall Park
Sports Ground
Wootton Hall (Pol HQ)
HIDCOTE RD
MANNINGTON GDS
TAPELEY GDS
GRANARY
NEWPORT
PAGNELL
ROAD
A508
RD
Hotel
Sports Field
School
Sch
B526
CASTLE BRIDGE CT
TATE GRO
HARDYDR
MERLIN GRO
HARRIER
PARK
KIMBLE CL
BRAEMAR
MELDON CL
STANFORD
PENVALE
THAMES RD
E
F
G
H
1
2
3
4
5
6
12
18
21

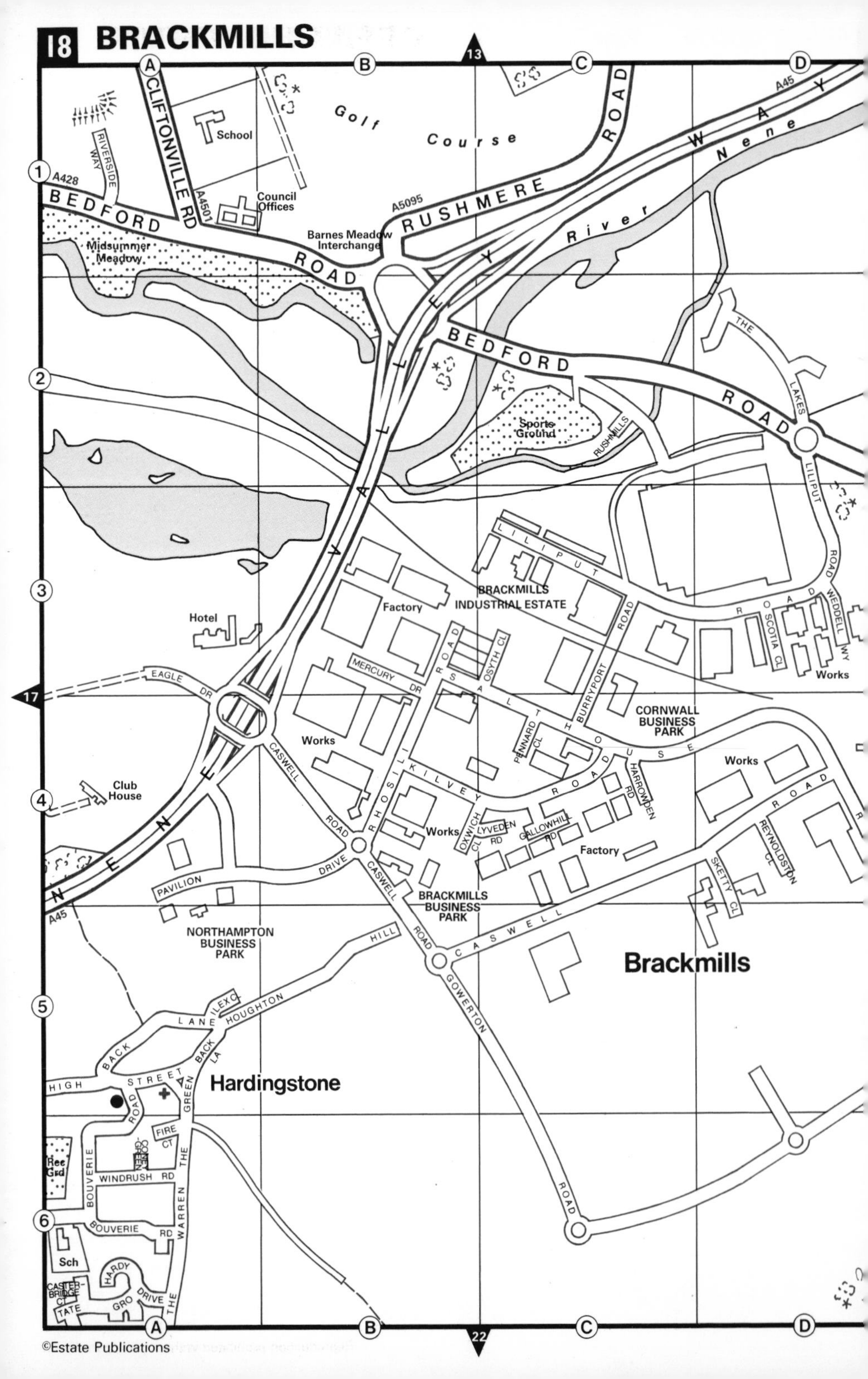

Golf Course
School
Council Offices
CLIFTONVILLE RD
RIVERSIDE WAY
A428
BEDFORD ROAD
A4501
A5095
RUSHMERE ROAD
Barnes Meadow Interchange
Midsummer Meadow
River Nene
NENE VALLEY WAY
A45
BEDFORD ROAD
THE LAKES
Sports Ground
RUSHMILLS
LILIPUT ROAD
Factory
BRACKMILLS INDUSTRIAL ESTATE
Hotel
MERCURY DR
OSYTH CL
BURRYPORT ROAD
SCOTIA CL
WEDDELL WY
Works
EAGLE DR
SALTHOUSE ROAD
CORNWALL BUSINESS PARK
PENNARD CL
CASWELL ROAD
RHOSILI ROAD
KILVEY ROAD
HARROWDEN RD
Club House
OXWICH CL
LYVEDEN RD
GALLOWHILL RD
PAVILION DRIVE
BRACKMILLS BUSINESS PARK
REYNOLDSTON CL
SKETTY CL
NORTHAMPTON BUSINESS PARK
HILL
CASWELL ROAD
GOWERTON ROAD
Brackmills
ILEX CT
HOUGHTON
BACK LANE
BACK LA
Hardingstone
HIGH STREET
GREEN
FIRE CT
COPPER GREEN
Rec Grd
BOUVERIE
WINDRUSH RD
BOUVERIE RD
THE WARREN
Sch
HARDY DRIVE
CASTERBRIDGE CT
TATE GRO
THE
13
17
22

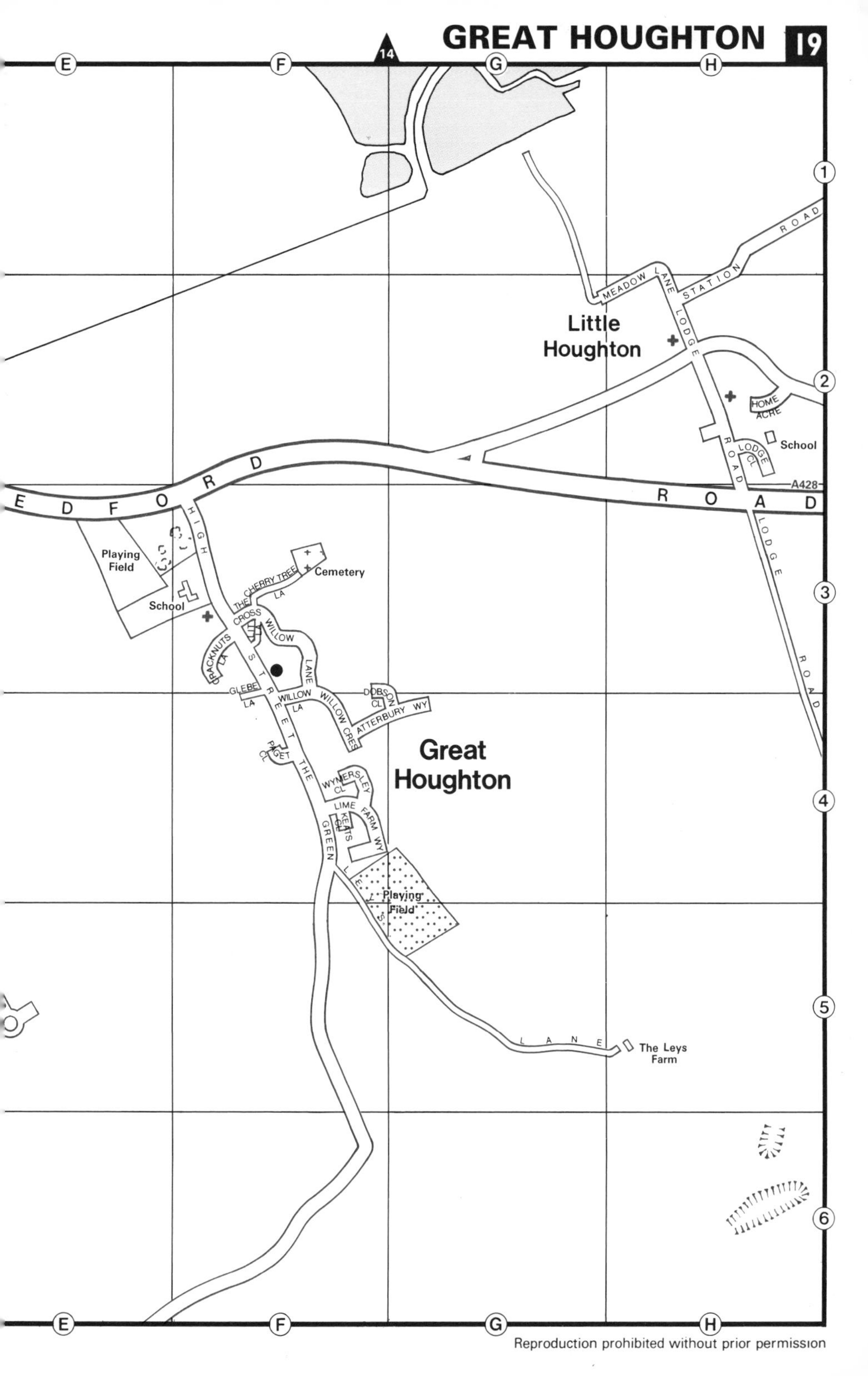
14
Little Houghton
MEADOW LANE
STATION ROAD
LODGE ROAD
HOME ACRE
LODGE CL
School
A428
BEDFORD ROAD
HIGH STREET
Playing Field
School
Cemetery
THE CHERRY TREE LA
CROSS
WILLOW LANE
CRACKNUTS LA
GLEBE LA
WILLOW LA
WILLOW CRES
DOBSON CL
ATTERBURY WY
PAGET CL
THE GREEN
Great Houghton
WYNERSLEY CL
LIME FARM WY
KEATS CL
LEYS LANE
Playing Field
The Leys Farm

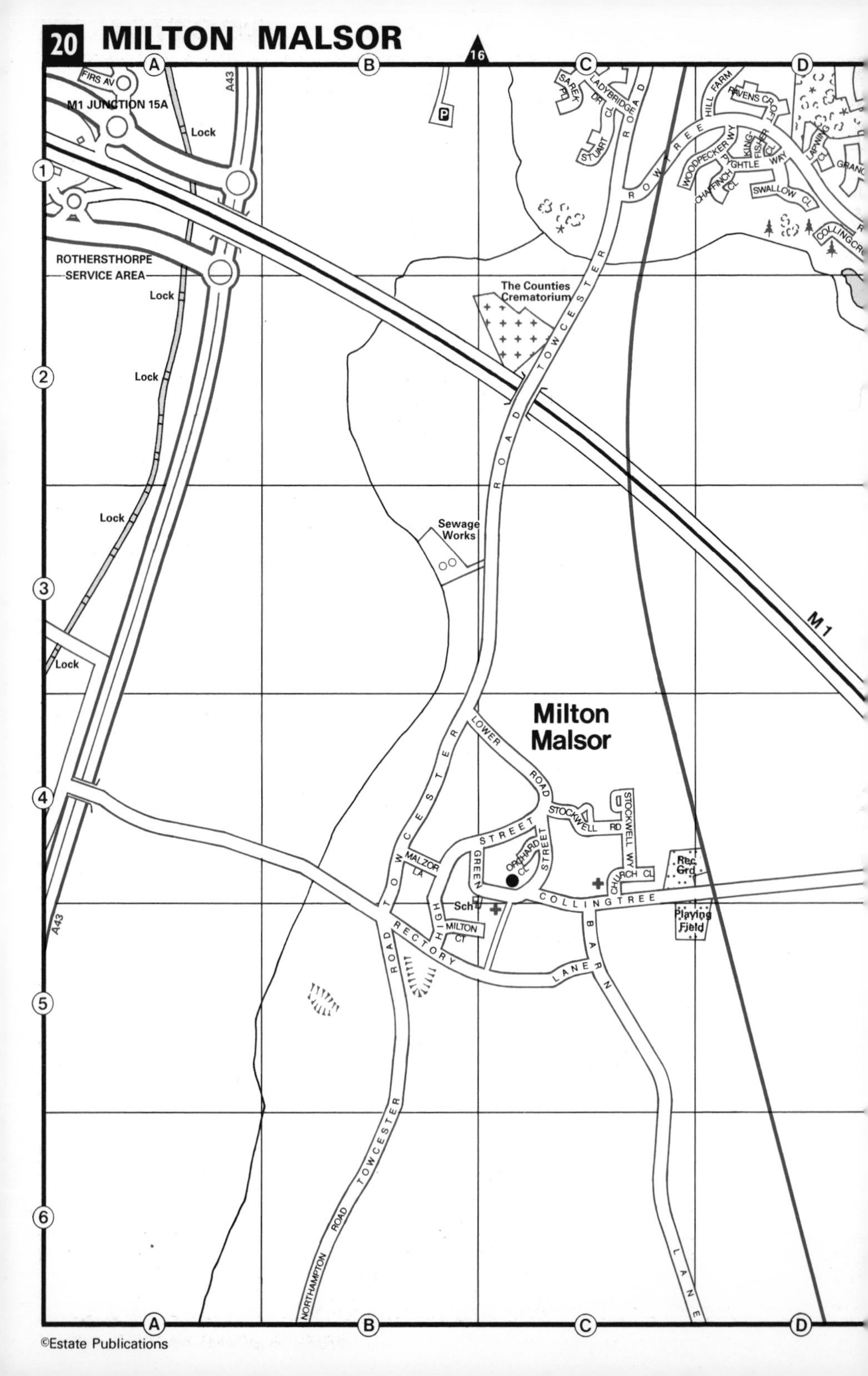
16
A
B
C
D
1
2
3
4
5
6
FIRS AV
M1 JUNCTION 15A
A43
Lock
ROTHERSTHORPE
SERVICE AREA
SAREK PL
LADYBRIDGE DR
STUART CL
TOWCESTER ROAD
ROWTREE ROAD
HILL FARM
RAVENS CROFT
WOODPECKER WY
KINGFISHER CL
PYGHTLE WAY
CHAFFINCH CL
SWALLOW CL
LAPWING CL
COLLINGCROFT
The Counties
Crematorium
Sewage
Works
M1
Milton
Malsor
LOWER ROAD
STOCKWELL RD
STOCKWELL WY
STREET
GREEN STREET
ORCHARD CL
MALZOR LA
CHURCH CL
Rec Grd
COLLINGTREE
Playing Field
Sch
HIGH
MILTON CT
RECTORY
LANE
BARN LANE
NORTHAMPTON ROAD
TOWCESTER ROAD

Merefield
Wootton Hall
Police H.Q.
School
Sch
Sports Field
NEWPORT PAGNELL ROAD
LONDON ROAD
A508
B526
HERMITAGE WAY
QUEBEC ROAD
HIGH STREET
WATER LANE
FARMCLOSE
Sports Ground
Cemy
Wootton
BERRY LANE
QUINTON ROAD
Collingtree Park
Golf Course
Nursing
Home
Collingtree
WATERING LANE
Pol Ho
Playing Field
Hotel
M1
JUNCTION 15

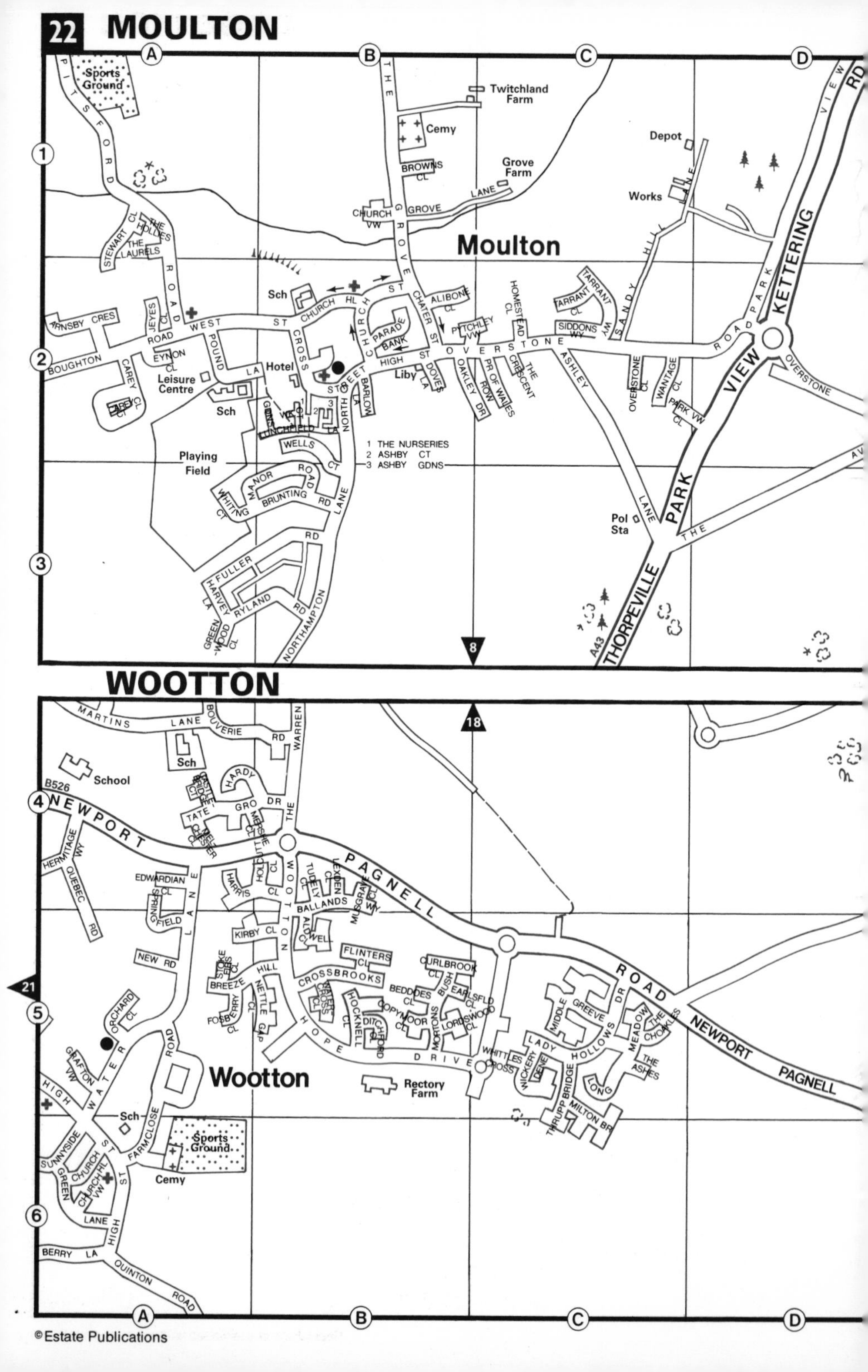
MOULTON
A
B
C
D
1
2
3
Sports Ground
PITSFORD ROAD
Twitchland Farm
Cemy
Depot
BROWNS CL
Grove Farm
GROVE LANE
Works
CHURCH VW
GROVE
THE GROVE
Moulton
STEWART CL
THE HOLLIES
THE LAURELS
SANDY HILL LANE
KETTERING
PARK VIEW
Sch
CHURCH HL
ST
CHATER ST
ALIBONE CL
HOMESTEAD CL
TARRANT WAY
TARRANT CL
ARNSBY CRES
JEYES CL
WEST ST
CROSS ST
CHURCH ST
PARADE
PYTCHLEY VW
SIDDONS WY
ROAD
BOUGHTON
ROAD
EYNON CL
POUND LA
Hotel
BANK
HIGH ST
OVERSTONE ROAD
ASHLEY LANE
OVERSTONE CL
WANTAGE CL
OVERSTONE
CAREY CL
Leisure Centre
NORTH ST
STREET
DOVES LA
OAKLEY DR
PR OF WALES ROW
THE CRESCENT
PARK VW CL
Liby
Sch
BARLOW LA
LUNCHFIELD LA
WELLS CT
1 THE NURSERIES
2 ASHBY CT
3 ASHBY GDNS
Playing Field
MANOR ROAD
WHITING CT
BRUNTING RD
LANE
RD
Pol Sta
THE AVENUE
THORPEVILLE
A43
FULLER
HARVEY LA
RYLAND RD
GREENWOOD CL
NORTHAMPTON
8
WOOTTON
18
MARTINS LANE
BOUVERIE RD
WARREN
Sch
School
HARDY DR
B526
NEWPORT PAGNELL ROAD
4
HERMITAGE WY
QUEBEC RD
TATE
GRO
THE
EDWARDIAN CL
HARRIS CL
HOLCUTT CL
WOOTTON
TUDELY CL
LEXDEN CL
MUSGRAVE WY
BALLANDS
SPRINGFIELD
LANE
KIRBY CL
ALDWELL CL
FLINTERS CL
CURLBROOK CL
NEW RD
STOKE
BREEZE HILL
CROSSBROOKS
BEDDOES CL
BUSH CL
EARLSFLD CL
NETTLE GAP
BERRY CL
FOSB
HOCKNELL CL
COPYMOOR CL
MORTONS
LORDSWOOD CL
21
5
ORCHARD CL
HOPE DRIVE
DITCHFORD CL
WHITTLES CROSS
LADY
MIDDLE GREEVE
DR
HOLLOWS
MEADOW
THE CHOWKLES
THE ASHES
NEWPORT PAGNELL
GRAFTON VW
WATER
ROAD
Wootton
Rectory Farm
WICKERY DENE
THRUPP BRIDGE
MILTON BR
LONG
HIGH
Sch
FARMCLOSE
Sports Ground
SUNNYSIDE
CHURCH HL VW
ST
GREEN
Cemy
6
LANE
HIGH ST
BERRY LA
QUINTON ROAD

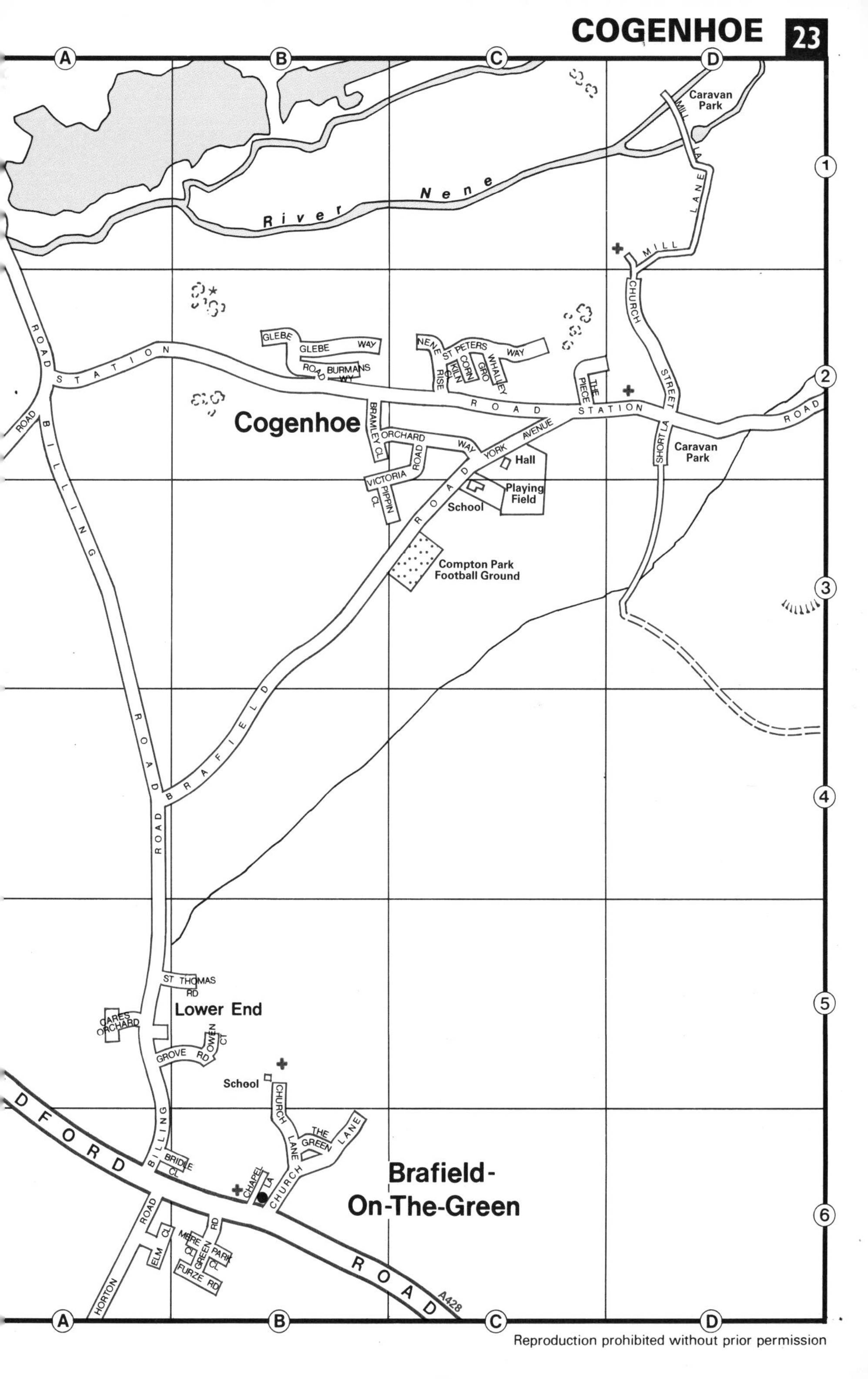
Cogenhoe
Lower End
Brafield-On-The-Green
River Nene
Caravan Park
Caravan Park
Hall
Playing Field
School
School
Compton Park Football Ground
STATION ROAD
BILLING ROAD
BRAFIELD ROAD
MILL LANE
CHURCH STREET
SHORT LA
GLEBE WAY
GLEBE ROAD
BURMANS WY
NENE RISE
ST PETERS WAY
KILN CL
CORN GRO
WHALLEY
THE PIECE
BRAMLEY CL
ORCHARD WAY
ORCHARD ROAD
VICTORIA RD
PIPPIN CL
YORK AVENUE
ST THOMAS RD
CARES ORCHARD
GROVE RD
OWEN CT
BRIDLE CL
CHAPEL LA
CHURCH LANE
THE GREEN
HORTON ROAD
ELM CL
MERE CL
GREEN PARK CL
FURZE RD
A428

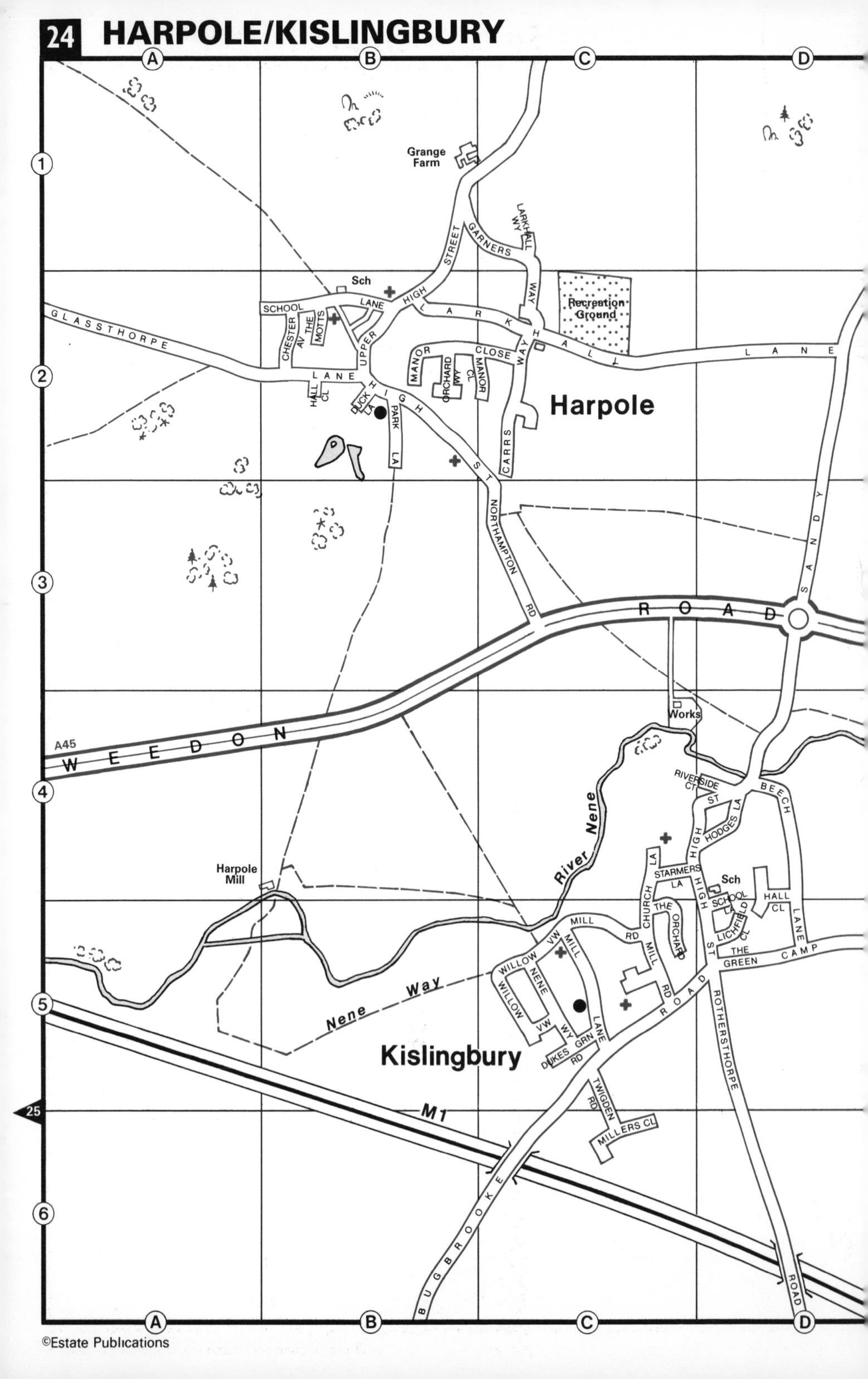
A
B
C
D
1
2
3
4
5
6
Grange Farm
Sch
Recreation Ground
Harpole
GLASSTHORPE
SCHOOL LANE
CHESTER AV
THE MOTTS
UPPER HIGH ST
HIGH STREET
GARNERS WAY
LARKHALL WAY
LARK HALL LANE
MANOR CLOSE
ORCHARD WY
MANOR CL
HALL CL
DUCK LA
PARK LA
CARRS WAY
NORTHAMPTON RD
SANDY LANE
WEEDON ROAD
A45
Works
River Nene
Harpole Mill
RIVERSIDE CT
BEECH LA
HIGH ST
HODGES LA
CHURCH LA
STARMERS LA
Sch
SCHOOL LA
HALL CL
HALL LANE
THE ORCHARD
LICHFIELD CL
MILL RD
MILL LANE
CAMP
THE GREEN
WILLOW VW
NENE WY
DUKES GRN
DUKES RD
Nene Way
Kislingbury
ROTHERSTHORPE ROAD
TWIGDEN RD
MILLERS CL
M1
BUGBROOKE ROAD
25

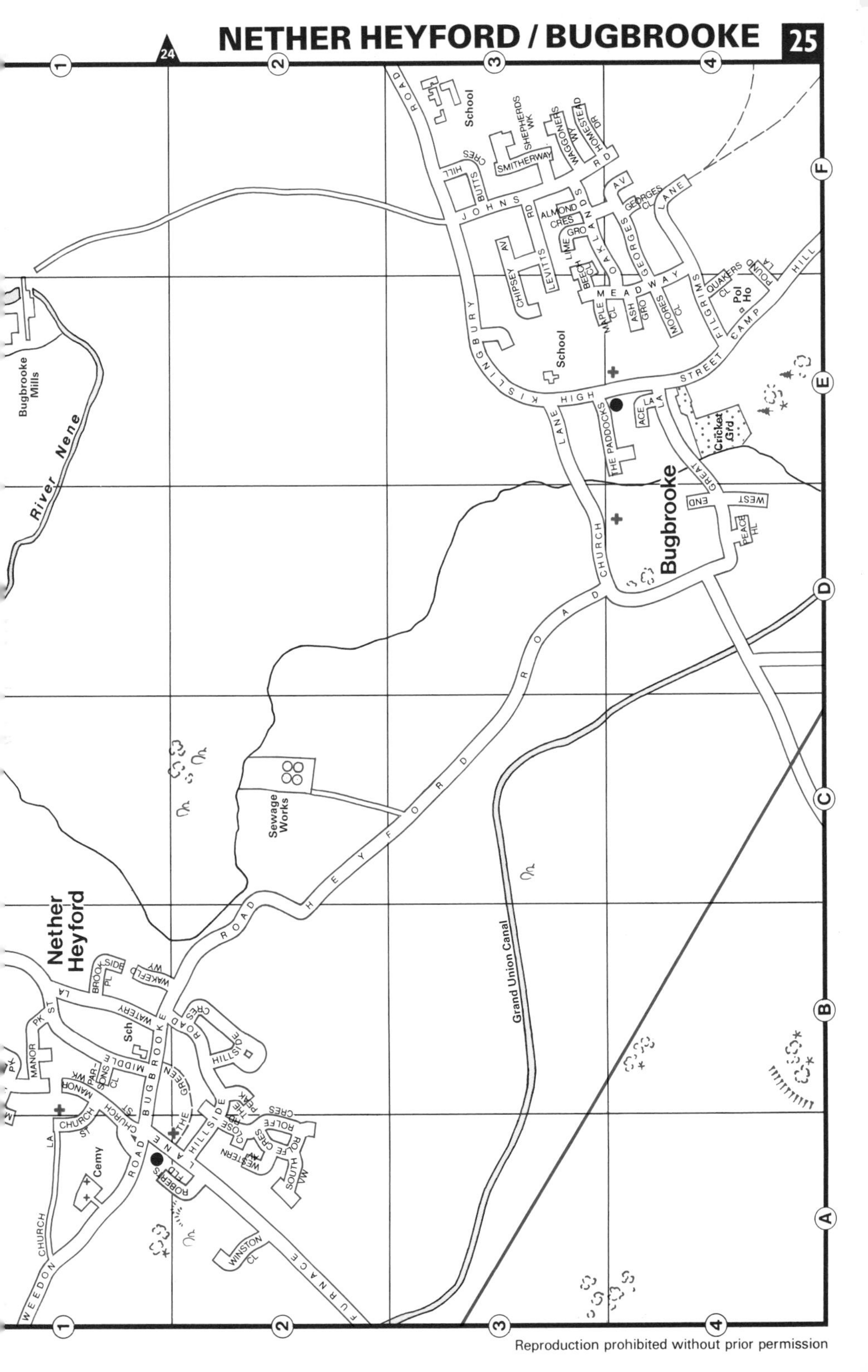

Bugbrooke
Nether Heyford
River Nene
Bugbrooke Mills
Grand Union Canal
Sewage Works
School
Sch
Cemy
Cricket Grd
Pol Ho
HEYFORD ROAD
KISLINGBURY ROAD
JOHNS RD
HIGH STREET
CHURCH LANE
GREAT LANE
WEST END
PEACE HL
THE PADDOCKS
ACE LA
FILGRIMS
QUAKERS CL
POUND LA
CAMP HILL
MEADWAY
OAKLANDS RD
GEORGES AV
GEORGES CL
LANE
MOORES CL
ASH GRO
MAPLE CL
BEECH CL
LIME GRO
ALMOND CRES
LEVITTS RD
CHIPSEY AV
BUTTS HILL CRES
SMITHERWAY
SHEPHERDS WK
WAGGONERS WY
HOMESTEAD DR
BROOKSIDE PL
WAKEFLD WY
WATERY LA
MANOR PK
ST
MIDDLE ST
PARSONS CL
MANOR WK
CHURCH ST
CHURCH LA
CHURCH ROAD
WEEDON ROAD
BUGBROOKE ROAD
THE GREEN
HILLSIDE CRES
HILLSIDE
THE PEAK
ROSE CT
ROLFE CRES
WESTERN AV
SOUTH VW
ROBERTS FLD
WINSTON CL
FURNACE LANE
A
B
C
D
E
F
1
2
3
4
24

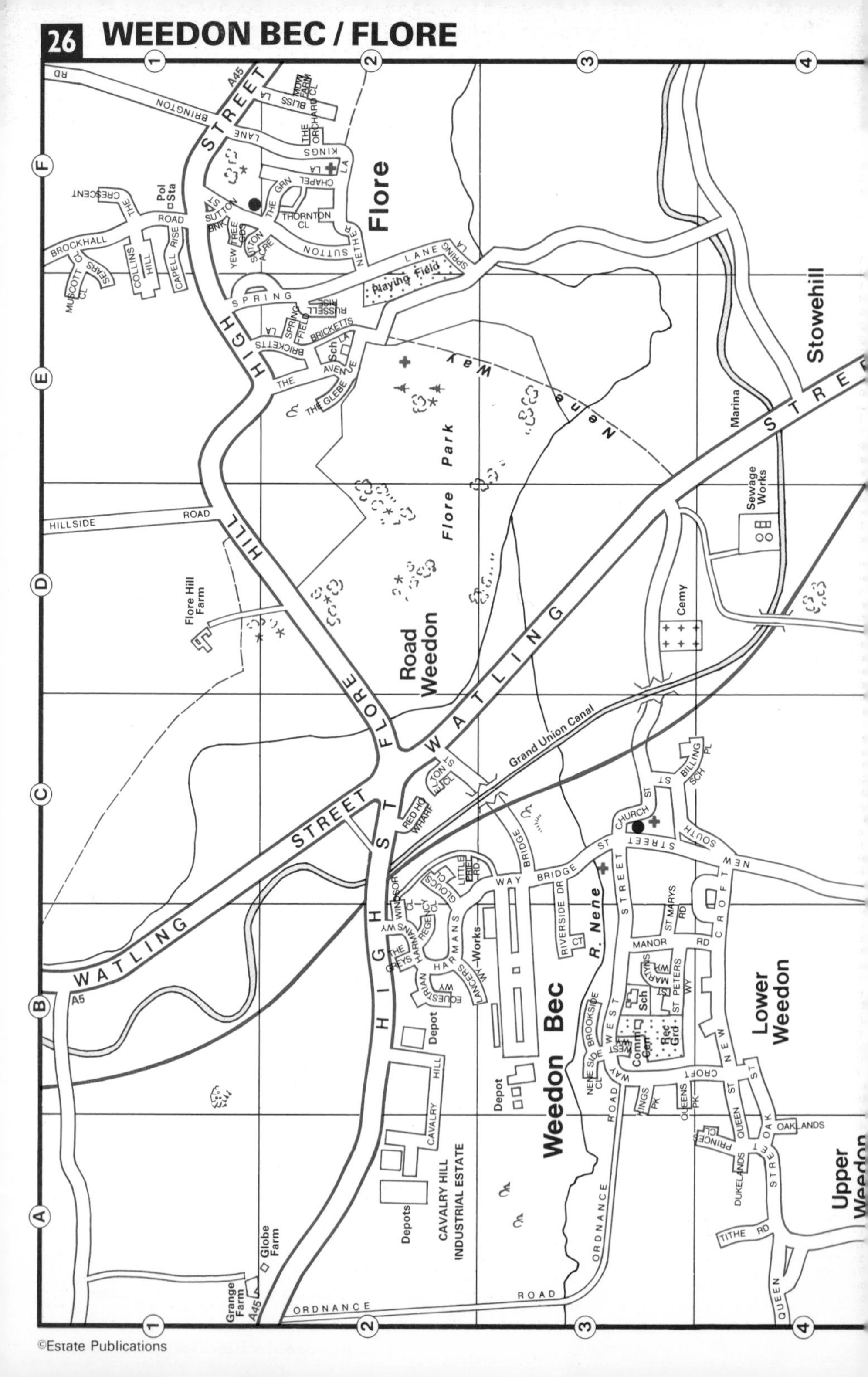
Flore
Flore Park
Road Weedon
Weedon Bec
Lower Weedon
Upper Weedon
Stowehill
HIGH STREET
WATLING STREET
HILL
FLORE
BRINGTON RD
BROCKHALL ROAD
HILLSIDE ROAD
SPRING LANE
SUTTON
KINGS LA
CHAPEL LA
THE GRN
THORNTON CL
NETHER LA
BLISS LA
MDW FARM
THE ORCHARD CL
THE CRESCENT
Pol Sta
COLLINS HILL
CAPELL RISE
MUSCOTT CL
SEARS CL
YEW TREE CL
SUTTON ACRE
Playing Field
RUSSELL RISE
SPRING FIELD
BRICKETTS LA
THE AVENUE
Sch
THE GLEBE
Nene Way
Marina
Sewage Works
Cemy
Flore Hill Farm
Grand Union Canal
BILLING PL
SCH ST
CHURCH ST
SOUTH STREET
BRIDGE ST
WAY
BRIDGE
NEW CROFT
RED HO WHARF
ELTON CL
LITTLE PRIEL RD
GLOUCS CL
WINDSOR CL
REGENCY CL
HARMANS WAY
THE GREYS
EQUESTRIAN WY
LANCERS WAY
Works
Depot
RIVERSIDE DR
RIVERSIDE CT
R. Nene
ST MARYS RD
MANOR RD
MARTYNS WY
ST PETERS WY
BROOKSIDE
WEST ST
Sch
Comm Cen
Rec Grd
NENE SIDE CL
WEST WAY
KINGS PK
QUEENS PK
QUEEN ST
OAK ST
OAKLANDS
PRINCES CL
DUKELANDS
TITHE RD
QUEEN
ORDNANCE ROAD
CAVALRY HILL
CAVALRY HILL INDUSTRIAL ESTATE
Depots
Globe Farm
Grange Farm
A45
A5

A - Z INDEX TO STREETS
with Postcodes

Index includes some
es for which there is
ficient space on the maps.
e names are preceded by
and are followed by the
st adjoining thoroughfare.

y Rd. NN4 17 E3
y St. NN5 12 B5
y Ter. NN5 12 A5
ts Way. NN5 11 H6
dare Rd. NN5 12 B3
gton Av. NN1 13 F4
gton Gro. NN1 13 F3
gton Pk Cres. NN3 14 A3
gton Sq. NN1 5 F2
gton St. NN1 5 D3
orpe Av. NN2 7 E4
.a. NN7 25 E4
La. NN2 6 A4
ns Av. NN1 13 F4
son Rd. NN3 13 H1
ecroft Ct. NN2 6 C6
side Pl. NN1 5 B3
t Rd. NN1 13 F4
te Way. NN6 4 A3
s Rd. NN2 12 D3
dale Clo. NN2 7 F6
ee Rd. NN3 7 F5
ny Rd. NN1 13 H4
t Pl. NN1 5 E2
n Pl. NN1 5 E3
nbe Rd. NN1 5 E1
Ct. NN3 8 D4
ley Clo. NN5 10 D4
ell Clo. NN4 22 B5
ndra Rd. NN1 5 F2
d St. NN1 13 F5
ne Clo. NN3 22 B2
l Clo. NN3 9 G4
one Rd. NN6 4 B4
Rd. NN1 13 G4
Yard. NN1 5 C2
St. NN5 12 B5
nd Cres. NN7 25 F3
e Way. NN5 10 C1
e Clo. NN5 10 C2
rp Rd. NN5 12 B5
rp St. NN1 5 B2
Clo. NN3 9 G5
eside Clo. NN3 8 B5
idge Clo. NN4 16 C5
St. NN1 5 C3
a Way. NN3 7 G3
Ct. NN5 10 C2
sley Clo. NN3 14 B5
l Way. NN4 17 G6
ebarn Clo. NN4 21 F4
edore Clo. NN2 6 D5
aine Clo. NN5 10 B3
ur Ct. NN3 8 C5
ur Vw Ct. NN3 8 C4
angel Rd. NN4 16 C3
angel Sq,
changel Rd. NN4 16 C3
ers Clo. NN2 6 B4
gton Rd. NN1 13 G4
e St. NN5 12 A4
Clo. NN5 10 C3
ry Rd. NN3 9 E5
ale. NN2 6 A4
d Rd. NN2 12 D3
by Cres. NN3 22 A2
y Head Rd. NN4 16 C2
r St. NN2 12 D2
n Rd. NN1 13 F4
del St. NN1 5 B1
t. NN1 12 D4
Gro. NN2 6 B4
Gro. NN7 25 E4
a. NN4 21 E4
ise. NN2 6 D3
t. NN1 12 D4
ree Way. NN5 11 E5
ow Rd. NN4 16 D3
urnham Rd. NN1 13 G3
y Ct. NN3 22 B2
y Gdns. NN3 22 B2
Ashcroft Clo. NN5 10 D3
Ashcroft Gdns. NN3 13 H1
Ashley La. NN3 22 C2
Ashley Way. NN3 14 C1
Ashpole Spinney. NN4 16 A4
Ashwood Rd. NN5 11 E5
Aspen Clo. NN3 9 G6
Aster Clo. NN3 14 B5
Aston Rise. NN5 10 D4
Atlee Clo. NN3 8 A5
Atterbury Way. NN4 19 F4
Auctioneers Ct. NN1 17 G1
Auctioneers Way. NN1 17 G1
Augusta Av. NN4 21 E2
Austin St. NN1 13 E4
Austins Yd. NN6 4 B3
Avebury Way. NN4 17 E6
Aviemore Gdns. NN4 16 B5
Avignon Clo. NN5 10 C2
Avon Dri. NN5 11 G3
Axe Head Rd. NN4 16 C2
Aynho Cres. NN2 6 D4
Aynho Wk. NN2 6 D4
Azalea Clo. NN3 14 B5
Back La. NN4 18 A5
Badby Clo. NN2 7 E5
Badgers Wk. NN2 6 B4
Bagnall Dri. NN4 16 A5
Bailiff St. NN1 5 D1
Baird Av. NN5 16 A1
Baker St. NN2 12 C3
Bakewell Clo. NN4 16 C6
Baldwin Clo. NN3 8 A5
Balfour Rd. NN2 12 D2
Ballands Way. NN4 22 B4
Balmoral Clo. NN6 4 C3
Balmoral Rd. NN2 12 D2
Banbury Clo. NN4 16 B4
Banbury La. NN4 16 A5
Bank Vw. NN4 21 E1
Bankside. NN2 7 F6
Bants La. NN5 11 F5
Bardon Clo. NN4 16 B3
Baring Rd. NN5 12 B4
Barker Rd. NN6 4 B3
Barley Hill Rd. NN3 8 D2
Barley La. NN2 6 B4
Barlow La. NN3 22 B2
Barn Cnr. NN4 21 F4
Barn La. NN7 20 C5
Barn Owl Clo. NN4 16 D6
Barn Way. NN5 11 E1
Barnard Clo. NN5 11 E4
Barnet Clo. NN4 16 D4
Barnfield Clo. NN2 6 C5
Barnhill Sq. NN3 9 E3
Barnstaple Clo. NN3 14 C4
Barnwell Rd. NN2 6 D5
Baron Av. NN6 4 B1
Barons Way. NN2 6 B5
Baronson Gdns. NN1 13 G4
Barrack Rd. NN1 12 D3
Barry Rd. NN1 13 G5
Basil Clo. NN4 21 G3
Baukewell Clo. NN3 8 C6
Baunhill Clo. NN3 14 B5
Beacon Ct. NN4 16 B3
Beaconsfield Ter. NN1 13 E4
Beaufort Dri. NN5 11 E3
Beaumont Dri. NN3 9 F6
Beaune Clo. NN5 10 C3
Beauvais Ct. NN5 10 C2
Beckett Way. NN3 8 A5
Bective Rd. NN2 6 D6
Beddoes Clo. NN4 22 B5
Bedford Pl. NN1 5 E3
Bedford Rd. NN1 5 E4
Bedford Rd. NN4 18 C2
Bedford Rd. NN7 23 A5
Beech Av. NN3 13 G1
Beech Clo. NN7 25 E3
Beech Gro. NN3 8 B4
Beech La. NN7 24 D4
Beechcroft Gdns. NN3 13 G1
Beechwood Dri. NN3 14 C2
Beechwood Dri. NN5 11 E5
Beeston Av. NN3 14 D3
Belfield Clo. NN3 7 H6
Belfry La. NN4 21 E3
Bellropes Sq. NN3 15 H1
Belstead Rd. NN3 14 B5
Belton Clo. NN4 17 F6
Belvedere Clo. NN5 11 H5
Belvoir Clo. NN5 10 D2
Bembridge Dri. NN2 12 C2
*Benjamin Sq,
Plantagenet Sq. NN4 16 C3
Bentley Clo. NN3 9 G5
Bergerac Clo. NN5 10 C1
Berkeley Dri. NN1 13 F6
Bern Side. NN4 16 D3
Berry Clo. NN6 4 A2
Berry La. NN4 22 A6
Berrydale. NN3 9 H5
Berrywood Rd. NN5 10 B4
Bestwell Ct. NN3 15 E4
Beverley Cres. NN3 14 A2
Bibury Cres. NN3 8 B4
Bidders Clo. NN1 17 G1
Bideford.Clo. NN3 14 B4
Billing Brook Rd. NN3 8 C4
Billing La. NN3 9 F3
Billing Rd. NN1 5 F3
Billing Rd. NN7 23 A2
Billing School Pl. NN7 26 C4
Billington St. NN1 13 F4
Birch Barn Way. NN2 6 B4
Birchfield Cres. NN3 14 B2
Birchfield Rd. NN1 13 G3
Birchfield Rd East. NN3 13 H2
Birds Hill Rd. NN3 8 D6
Birds Hill Wk. NN3 14 D1
Birkdale Clo. NN2 7 F6
Bishops Dri. NN2 6 B6
Bitten Ct. NN3 8 C6
Black Lion Hill. NN1 5 A3
Blackberry La. NN4 16 C2
Blackmore La. NN4 21 G3
Blackthorn. NN3 9 F5
Blackthorn Rd. NN3 9 F5
Blackwell Hill. NN4 16 C6
Bladon Clo. NN3 8 A5
Blakesley Clo. NN2 6 D4
Bledlow Rise. NN4 16 C6
Blenheim Rd. NN4 17 E4
Bliss La. NN7 26 F2
Blossac Ct. NN5 10 B3
Blossom Way. NN3 15 E2
Bluebell Ct. NN3 14 B5
Boarden Clo. NN3 7 G2
Bobtail Ct. NN5 11 F3
Bollinger Clo. NN5 10 C3
Bondfield Av. NN2 7 E6
Booth La Nth. NN3 8 B4
Booth La Sth. NN3 14 B1
Booth Meadow Ct. NN3 8 C4
Booth Rise. NN3 8 B4
Bordeaux Clo. NN5 10 C3
Bostock Av. NN1 13 F4
Bosworth Clo. NN4 16 D4
Botmead Rd. NN3 9 G5
Bougainvillea Dri. NN3 14 B5
Boughton Grn La. NN3 7 F2
Boughton Grn Rd. NN2 6 D5
Boughton La. NN3 7 F2
Boughton Rd,
Moulton. NN3 22 A2
Boughton Rd,
Moulton Pk. NN3 7 F2
Bourne Cres.NN5 11 G2
Bourton Clo. NN4 16 C5
Bouverie Rd. NN4 18 A6
Bouveries Wk. NN1 13 F5
Bow Ct. NN4 16 B3
Bowden Rd. NN5 12 B6
Bowmans Clo. NN4 16 A4
Bowthorpe Clo. NN3 14 C5
Brackenhill Clo. NN2 7 F6
Brackley Clo. NN2 6 D4
Bradden Clo. NN2 6 D4
Bradmoor Ct. NN3 9 F4
Bradshaw St. NN1 5 C2
Braemar Cres. NN4 17 F6
Brafield Rd. NN7 23 B4
Bramble End. NN4 16 C6
Bramcote Dri. NN3 14 D3
Bramhall Rise. NN5 10 D4
Bramley Clo. NN7 23 B2
Bramley Gro. NN3 15 F1
Brampton. NN3 7 G4
Branksome Av. NN2 12 C2
Brashland Dri. NN4 21 G2
Brayford Clo. NN3 14 A5
Brecon St.NN5 12 B4
Breeze Hill. NN4 22 A5
Brendon Clo. NN3 14 B4
Bretton Clo. NN5 10 D2
Briar Hill Rd.NN4 17 E3
Briar Hill Wk. NN4 17 E3
Brick Kiln La. NN2 12 D3
Bricketts La. NN7 26 E2
Brickwell Ct. NN3 15 E3
Brickyard. NN3 7 H3
Bridge Ct. NN3 9 F5
Bridge St. NN1 5 C3
Bridge St. NN7 26 C3
Bridgewater Dri. NN3 14 A4
Bridle Clo. NN7 23 A6
Brill Clo. NN4 16 A5
Brindlestone Clo. NN4 16 A4
Brington Rd. NN7 26 F1
Briton Gdns. NN3 13 H3
Briton Rd. NN3 13 H3
Brittons Dri. NN3 9 E2
Broad St. NN1 5 C2
Broad St. NN6 4 B3
Broadhurst Dri. NN3 15 E4
Broadmead Av. NN3 13 G1
Broadway. NN1 13 G2
Broadway East. NN3 13 G2
Brocade Clo. NN4 16 C3
Brockhall Clo. NN2 7 E5
Brockhall Rd. NN2 7 E5
Brockhall Rd. NN7 26 F1
Brockton St. NN2 12 D2
Brockwood Clo. NN5 10 C2
Bromford Clo. NN3 15 E4
Brook La. NN5 12 A3
Brook St. NN1 12 C4
Brookfield Rd. NN2 13 F1
Brookland Cres. NN1 13 G2
Brookland Rd. NN1 13 G2
Brookside. NN7 26 B3
Brookside Mdw. NN5 11 G3
Brookside Pl. NN7 25 B1
*Broom Ct,
Hunsbarrow Rd. NN4 16 D3
Broomhill Cres. NN3 9 E3
Brough Clo. NN5 10 C3
Broughton Pl. NN3 8 A6
Brownlow Ct. NN3 8 C5
Browns Clo. NN3 22 B1
Browns Way. NN1 17 H1
Bruce St. NN5 11 H5
Brundall Clo. NN3 14 C5
Brunel Dri. NN5 16 A1
Brunswick Pl. NN1 13 F4
Brunting Rd. NN3 22 B3
Buchanan Clo. NN4 17 E3
Buckingham Clo. NN4 21 E1
Bugbrooke Rd,
Kislingbury. NN7 24 B6
Bugbrooke Rd,
Nether Heyford. NN7 25 B1
Bunting Rd. NN2 12 D2
Burford Av. NN3 8 B4
Burmans Way. NN7 23 B2
Burns Clo. NN6 4 C3
Burns St. NN1 13 E4
Burrows Ct. NN3 8 C5
Burryport Rd. NN4 18 C4
Burtram Clo. NN3 14 C2
Burwood Rd. NN3 13 H1
Bush Hill. NN3 14 A2
Bushland Rd. NN3 14 B1
Butchers La. NN2 6 D1
Buttermere Clo. NN3 8 B5
Butts Croft Clo. NN4 21 F2
Butts Hill Cres. NN7 25 F3
Butts Rd. NN4 21 F2
Byfield Rd. NN5 12 B6
Byron St. NN2 13 F2
Calder Grn. NN5 11 G2
Calstock Clo. NN3 14 B4
Camberley Clo. NN3 15 F2
Camborne Clo. NN4 17 E4
Cambria Cres. NN3 14 A2
Cambridge St. NN2 12 C3
Camelot Way. NN5 10 C4
Cameron Clo. NN5 11 G5
Cameron Cres. NN5 11 G5
Camp Hill. NN7 25 E4
Camp La. NN7 24 D5
Campbell Sq. NN1 5 D1
Campbell Sq. NN6 4 A3
Campbell St. NN1 5 C1
Campion Ct. NN3 15 F2
Camrose Rd. NN5 12 B4
Candace Ct. NN5 11 G3
Candleford. NN3 9 F5
Canona Wk. NN2 6 B6
Capell Rise. NN7 26 F1
Cardigan Clo. NN5 12 A3
Cardinal Clo. NN4 21 E1
Cares Orchard. NN7 23 A5
Carey Clo. NN3 22 A2
Carey Ct. NN3 22 A2
Carline Ct. NN3 8 B5
Carlton Gdns. NN2 13 F2
Carlton Rd. NN2 13 F2
Carlyle Av. NN5 11 G5
Carousel Way. NN3 14 D5
Carrington Gdns. NN3 14 D3
Carrs Way. NN7 24 C2
Cartmel Pl. NN3 8 A6
Cartwright Rd. NN2 12 C2
Castilian St. NN1 5 E3
Castilian Ter. NN1 5 E3
Castle Av. NN5 11 E4
Castle Bush. NN5 11 E4
Castle Clo. NN5 11 E4
Castle Hill. NN1 5 B2
Castle St. NN1 5 B2
Castlebridge Ct. NN4 22 A4
Caswell Rd. NN4 18 B4
Catesby Clo. NN2 7 E5
Cattle Hill. NN3 15 G1
Cattle Market Rd. NN1 17 F1
Catton Cres. NN2 6 A5
Cauldecott Clo. NN4 16 A4
Cavalry Hill. NN7 26 A2
Cavendish Dri. NN3 14 B5
Cecil Rd. NN2 12 D2
Cedar Ct. NN5 11 H4
Cedar Rd. NN1 13 G3
Cedar Rd East. NN3 13 H2
Cedrus Ct. NN2 6 A4
Celeborn Pl. NN3 9 F4
Central Av. NN2 6 C3
Chadstone Av. NN2 7 E4
Chadwick Gdns. NN5 11 F2
Chaffinch Clo. NN4 20 D1
Chalcombe Av. NN2 6 C4
Chalcombe Rd. NN2 6 D5
Chalk La. NN1 5 A3
Chantry Clo. NN3 9 F6
Chapel Grn. NN5 12 A1
Chapel La,
Brafield. NN7 23 B6
Chapel La, Flore. NN7 26 F2
Chapel Pl. NN1 5 F1
*Chapel Row,
Windsor Ct. NN3 15 G1
Chardonnay Clo. NN5 10 C2
Charles St. NN1 5 E1
Charlton Clo. NN2 6 D4
Charnwood Av. NN3 14 B1
Chartwell Av. NN3 8 A4
Chater St. NN3 22 B2
Chatsworth Av. NN3 8 D4
Chaucer St. NN2 13 F2
Cheddar Clo. NN5 11 F5
Chedworth Clo. NN3 15 H1
Chelfham Clo. NN3 14 B4
Chelmsford Clo. NN4 17 E3
Chepstow Clo. NN5 12 B4
Cheriton Way. NN3 14 A5
Cherry Blossom Clo.
NN3 15 F1
Cherry Clo. NN3 14 B2
Cherry Lodge Rd. NN3 9 F5
Cherry Tree La. NN4 19 F3
Cherwell Grn. NN5 11 H3
Chesham Rise. NN3 9 F5

Chester Av. NN7 24 B2
Chestnut Av.NN4 21 G3
Chestnut Rd. NN3 13 G2
Chestnut Ter. NN3 13 H2
Cheviot Ct. NN4 16 B3
Chewton Clo. NN5 11 G5
Cheyne Wk. NN1 5 F4
Chillwell Ct. NN3 14 D3
Chiltern Av. NN5 11 F4
Chiltern Clo. NN5 11 F4
Chiltern Way. NN5 11 G4
Chipsey Av. NN1 13 H5
Chipsey Av. NN7 25 F3
Christchurch Rd. NN1 13 G4
Chulmleigh Wk. NN3 14 A5
Church Clo. NN7 20 C4
Church Grn. NN5 11 H2
Church Hill. NN3 22 B2
Church Hill. NN4 22 A6
Church La. NN1 5 C1
Church La. NN3 15 E4
Church La,
Brafield. NN7 23 B6
Church La,
Bugbrooke. NN7 25 D3
Church La,
Kislingbury. NN7 24 C5
Church La,
Nether Heyford. NN7 25 A1
Church St. NN2 6 D1
Church St. NN3 22 B2
Church St,
Cogenhoe. NN7 23 D2
Church St,
Nether Heyford. NN7 25 A1
Church St,
Weedon Bec. NN7 26 C3
Church Vw. NN3 22 B1
Church Vw. NN4 22 A6
Church Wk. NN3 15 F1
Church Way. NN3 14 B3
Churchill Av. NN3 8 A5
Churchill Rd. NN6 4 B3
Cinnamon Clo. NN4 21 G2
Circus End. NN5 11 E3
Cissbury Rd. NN4 16 C2
Clannel Rd. NN4 16 D5
Clare Clo. NN6 4 C3
Clare St. NN1 13 E4
Claregate. NN4 17 E6
Clarence Av. NN2 12 D2
Clarke Ct. NN6 4 B3
Clarke Rd. NN1 13 G3
Claughton Rd. NN4 17 G2
Clayfield Clo. NN3 7 H3
Claystones NN4 16 B4
Clee Rise.NN5 11 F4
Cleveland Pl. NN4 16 D3
Cliftonville. NN1 13 F6
Cliftonville Ct. NN1 13 F6
Cliftonville Rd. NN1 13 F6
Clinton Rd. NN4 17 E3
Clipston Field Pl. NN3 15 G2
Clipstow Way. NN5 11 F3
Clocktower Ct. NN3 8 C3
Close Rd. NN7 25 A2
Cloutsham St. NN1 5 E1
Clover La. NN2 6 B3
Clumber Dri. NN3 14 C4
Coaching Wk. NN3 14 B1
Cobblestone Ct. NN4 16 A4
Coblin Clo. NN3 15 E2
Coldstream La. NN4 17 H5
Coleraine Clo. NN2 6 B5
College Field Clo. NN3 9 G6
College St. NN1 5 C3
College St Mws. NN1 5 C3
Collingcroft Clo. NN4 20 D1
Collingdale Rd. NN3 14 B1
Collingtree Rd. NN7 20 C4
Collingwood Rd. NN1 13 F2
Collins Hill. NN7 26 F1
Collins St. NN1 13 G5
Collmead Ct. NN3 9 F5
Collyweston Rd. NN3 9 G4
Colonial Dri. NN4 21 F3
Colwyn Rd. NN1 13 E4
Commercial St. NN1 5 C4
Compton Clo. NN6 4 B4
Compton St. NN1 5 B1
Compton Way. NN6 4 B4
Conduit La. NN1 5 D3
Coneygree Ct. NN3 15 F2
Coneygreen. NN4 18 A6
Coneywell Ct. NN3 14 D2
Conifer Rise. NN3 14 C2
Coniston Av. NN3 7 H6
Connnaught St. NN1 5 D1
Conway Clo. NN5 11 G2
Conyngham Rd. NN3 14 D2
Copper Leaf Clo. NN3 8 A3
Coppice Dri. NN3 7 G5
Copse Clo. NN2 6 A4
Copymoor Clo. NN4 22 B5
Corbieres Clo. NN5 10 C2
Cordon Clo. NN3 9 F6
Cordon Cres. NN6 4 C3
Corn Kiln. NN7 23 C2
Cornfield Clo. NN2 6 B4
Cornhill Clo. NN5 11 E1
Corran Clo. NN5 11 G4
Cosgrove Rd. NN2 6 D4
Cosgrove Way. NN2 6 D4
Cotswold Av. NN5 11 E3
Cottarville. NN3 14 B2
Cottage Clo. NN2 6 B5
Cottage Gdns. NN3 9 E6
Cottagewell Ct. NN3 14 D3
Cottesbrooke Gdns.
NN4 21 G1
Cottesmore Clo. NN5 11 E2
Cottingham Dri. NN3 7 H3
Cotton End. NN4 17 F2
Countess Rd. NN5 12 B4
Courteenhall Clo. NN2 7 E4
Coverack Clo. NN4 17 E4
Coverdale. NN2 6 A4
Covert Clo. NN2 6 B4
Covington St. NN1 13 G5
Cow Yd. NN2 6 B6
Cowgill Clo. NN3 9 F6
Cowley Clo. NN4 21 G2
Cowper Clo. NN6 4 C3
Cowper St. NN1 13 E4
Crab Tree Dri. NN3 9 E2
Cranbrooke Rd. NN2 12 D2
Cranford Rd. NN2 6 D6
Cranmere Av. NN1 13 H5
Cranstoun St. NN1 5 E1
Craven St. NN1 13 E4
Crawford Av. NN5 11 G4
Crediton Clo. NN3 14 B4
Crestline Ct. NN3 9 E4
Crestwood Gdns.NN3 8 D4
Crestwood Rd. NN3 8 C4
Cricklade Clo. NN3 14 B5
Crickley Cres. NN4 16 B2
Crispin St. NN1 5 B2
Crocket Clo. NN2 13 F1
Croft Way. NN7 26 B4
Crofters Clo. NN4 21 E1
Croftmeadow Ct. NN3 9 F5
Cromwell St. NN1 5 B1
Cross St. NN3 22 B2
Crossbrooks. NN4 22 B5
Croughton Clo. NN2 6 D4
Crow La. NN3 15 G4
Crowberry Av. NN3 8 A3
Crownsmead. NN4 16 A4
Crowthorpe. NN3 9 G4
Croxdale Clo. NN2 6 A4
Cubleigh Clo. NN3 8 A3
Cullahill Ct. NN4 16 B4
Culworth Cres. NN2 6 D4
Cumberland Av. NN3 7 H6
Cumbrae Dri. NN3 15 G1
Curlbrook Clo. NN4 22 B5
Currie Rd. NN2 12 C3
Cyclamen Clo. NN3 14 B5
Cypress Clo. NN3 8 C6
Cyril St. NN1 13 F5

Da Vinci. NN5 16 A1
Daimler Clo. NN3 9 G5
Dairy Mdw. NN3 8 D3
Dalestones. NN4 16 B4
Dallington Grn. NN5 12 A3
Dallington Pk Rd. NN5 12 A3
Dallington Rd. NN5 12 A3
Damson Dell. NN3 15 E3
Dane Ridge. NN5 11 E5
Danefield Rd. NN3 14 A2
Danes Back Dri. NN2 6 C6
Danes Camp Way. NN4 16 B3
Danetree Gdns. NN3 13 H2
Danewood Gdns. NN3 13 H1
Dapplestone Clo. NN4 16 A4
Darwin Wk. NN5 11 E3
Dayrell Rd. NN4 16 C4
Dayrell Sq. NN4 16 C4
Deacons Ct. NN3 9 G5
Deal Ct. NN1 12 D4
Deal St. NN1 12 D4
Deancourt Dri. NN5 10 D2
Deansway. NN3 9 G5
Debdale Rd. NN3 14 B1
Deer Park Rd. NN3 7 G3
Delamere Rd. NN4 17 F4
Delapre Cres. NN4 17 F3
Delapre Cres Rd. NN4 17 E3
Delapre St. NN4 17 E3
Dell Cres. NN3 9 F4
Delta Way. NN2 6 A4
Denbigh Rd. NN3 14 B5
Denmark Rd. NN1 5 F2
Denston Clo. NN4 17 E5
Derby Rd. NN1 13 F4
Derngate. NN1 5 D3
Derwent Clo. NN5 12 A2
Derwent Dri. NN5 11 H3
Devon Way. NN3 7 G4
Devonshire Clo. NN2 6 D2
Dickson Clo. NN4 16 C3
Dimock Sq. NN4 16 C3
Ditchford Clo. NN4 22 B5
Dobson Clo. NN4 19 G4
Doddington Rd. NN6 4 B3
Doddridge St. NN1 5 B3
Donellan Grn. NN3 8 D3
Donovan Ct. NN3 14 C4
Dore Clo. NN3 9 F4
Dorset Gdns. NN2 6 D6
Dorset Rd. NN2 6 D6
Douglas Rd. NN5 10 C4
Doves La. NN3 22 B2
Downsway. NN4 21 E2
Downthorpe End. NN6 4 B3
Downthorpe Hill. NN6 4 B4
Downward Clo. NN3 9 F6
Draycott Clo. NN3 14 C4
Drovers Wk. NN2 6 B4
Druids Way. NN3 7 G4
Drum La. NN1 5 C3
Drydale. NN3 7 H6
Dryden Rd. NN5 12 A4
Dryland Rd. NN3 14 A1
Dryleys Ct. NN3 9 E4
Drywell Ct. NN3 15 E3
Duck La. NN7 24 B2
Duckworth Dell. NN3 8 D3
Duke St. NN1 13 E4
Dukelands. NN7 26 A4
Dukes Grn Rd. NN7 24 C5
Dulce Rd. NN5 11 E4
Dulverton Rd. NN3 14 B4
Duncan Clo. NN3 7 F3
Dundee St. NN5 11 H5
Dunster St. NN1 5 E1
Duston Mill La. NN5 16 A1
Duston Rd. NN5 11 F5
Duston Wildes. NN5 10 D2
Dychurch La. NN1 5 D3

Eagle Dri. NN4 18 A3
Earl St. NN1 5 E1
Earls Barton Rd. NN29 4 E2
Earlsfield Clo. NN4 22 B5
East Bank. NN3 8 C3
East Bewick Rd. NN3 14 C4
East Butterfield Ct. NN3 8 D4
East Leys Ct. NN3 8 A2
East Mead Ct. NN3 15 E2
East Oval. NN5 11 H2
East Paddock Ct. NN3 9 E5
East Priors Ct. NN3 9 E6
East Rising. NN4 21 G2
East St. NN1 13 G5
Eastern Av Nth. NN2 7 E4
Eastern Av Sth. NN2 12 D1
Eastern Clo. NN2 7 E4
Eastfield Clo. NN5 11 E3
Eastfield Rd. NN4 17 F3
Eastfield Rd. NN5 10 D4
Eaton Rd. NN5 10 C3
Ecton Brook Rd. NN3 9 G6
Ecton Pk Rd. NN3 9 G6
Ecton St. NN1 5 F2
Eden Clo. NN3 8 A5
Edgehill Rd. NN5 11 F3
Edgemead Clo. NN3 8 C2
Edgemont Rd. NN3 14 C3
Edges Ct. NN3 8 A2
Edinburgh Rd.NN2 12 D2
Edison Dri. NN5 16 A1
Edith St. NN1 13 F5
Edwardian Clo. NN4 22 A4
Edwinstowe Clo. NN3 14 C4
Ekins Clo. NN3 14 B2
Eldean Rd. NN5 10 D3
Elderberry Ct. NN3 9 G6
*Eleonore Ho,
Buttermere Clo. NN3 8 B6
Elgin St. NN5 11 H5
Elizabeth Clo. NN6 4 B2
Elizabeth Wk. NN1 13 F5
Elizabeth Way. NN6 4 A2
Ellesmere Av. NN5 11 G5
Ellfield Ct. NN3 8 D6
Elm Clo. NN7 23 A6
Elm St. NN1 12 D4
Elmhurst Av. NN3 13 G1
Elmhurst Ct. NN3 13 G1
Elmington Rd. NN3 9 G4
Elmwood Wk. NN5 10 C2
Elton Clo. NN3 9 F4
Elton Clo. NN7 26 C2
Elwes Way. NN3 15 F1
Emerald Way. NN1 5 A3
Emley Clo. NN3 14 D2
Enfield Clo. NN5 10 C4
Ennerdale Clo. NN3 7 G6
Ennerdale Rd. NN3 7 G6
Entwood Dri. NN3 9 F4
Equestrian Way. NN7 26 B2
Ermine Rd. NN3 9 G4
Esher Ct. NN3 8 B5
Eskdale Av. NN3 8 A6
Essex St. NN2 12 C3
Ethel St. NN1 13 F5
Euston Rd. NN4 17 F2
Evenley Rd. NN2 6 D4
Everdon Clo NN2 7 E5
Evesham Ct. NN3 9 E2
Excalibur Clo. NN5 10 C4
Excelsior Gdns. NN5 10 C3
Exeter Pl. NN1 13 F5
Exmoor Clo. NN3 14 B4
Eynon Clo. NN3 22 A2

Fair Mile. NN2 6 B3
Fairfield Rd. NN2 13 G1
Fairground Way. NN3 14 C5
Fairhurst Way. NN6 4 B3
Fairmead Rise. NN2 6 A3
Fairway. NN2 13 E2
Falconers Rise. NN4 16 D6
Falcutt Way. NN2 7 E4
Fallow Wk. NN2 6 B3
Far Meadow Ct. NN3 8 C4
Faracre Ct. NN3 15 F2
Faraday Clo. NN5 16 A1
Faramere Pl. NN3 9 F4
Faringdon Ct. NN3 9 E2
Farm Broom Ct. NN3 8 D4
Farm Clo. NN2 6 B5
Farm Field Ct. NN3 8 C4
Farmclose Rd. NN4 22 A6
Farmhill Rd. NN3 9 E3
Farndon Clo. NN3 9 E4
Farnworth Clo. NN5 11 E3
Farraxton Sq. NN4 16 C4
Favell Way. NN3 14 B4
Fawsey Rd. NN4 17 F4
Faxton Clo. NN2 7 E5
Fellmead Rd. NN3 9 G4
Fengate Clo. NN3 9 G4
Ferndale Rd. NN3 14 B1
Fernie Field. NN3 8 A3
Ferris Row. NN3 14 D4
Fetter St. NN1 5 D4
Field Rose Sq. NN3 15 G1
Fieldmill Rd. NN3 15 F3
Fieldway. NN3 14 A2
Fienesgate. NN4 16 A5
Fife St. NN5 11 H5
Filleigh Way. NN3 14 A4
Fir Tree Wk. NN3 14 C1
Firbank Clo NN3 14 D3
Fire Ct. NN4 18 A6
Firs Av. NN4 16 A6
Firsview Dri. NN5 11 E3
Fish St. NN1 5 D3
Fishers Clo. NN3 15 F3
Fishponds Rd. NN3 15 E2
Fitzroy Pl. NN1 5 A2
Fitzroy Ter. NN1 5 C1
Five Acres Fold. NN4 16 C3
Flaxlands Ct. NN3 8 D6
Flaxwell Ct. NN3 14 D3
Fleetwind Dri. NN4 21 G2
Flintcombe Rise. NN3
Flinters Clo. NN4
Flore Hill. NN7
Florence Rd. NN1
Floribunda Dri. NN4
Forest Rd. NN4
Forfar St. NN5
Fort Pl. NN1
Fosberry Clo. NN4
Foskitt Ct. NN3
Foundry St. NN1
Fox Hill Rd. NN3
Foxcovert Rd. NN3
Foxendale Sq. NN3
Foxford Clo. NN4
Foxgrove Av. NN2
Foxwell Sq. NN3
Francis St. NN1
Franklin Cres. NN5
Franklin St. NN5
Fraser Rd. NN3
Freehold St. NN2
Freeschool St. NN1
Fremeaux Ter. NN2
Friars Av. NN4
Friars Clo. NN4
Friars Cres. NN4
Frosty Hollow. NN4
Fulford Dri. NN2
Fuller Rd. NN3
Fullerburn Ct. NN3
Fullingdale Rd. NN3
Furbur Ct. NN3
Furnace La. NN7
*Furze Ct,
Hunsbarrow Rd. NN4
Furze Rd. NN7
Furze Wk. NN2
Fuchsia Clo. NN3
Fylingdale. NN2

Gadesby Ct. NN3
Galahad Ct. NN5
Galaine Clo. NN4
Gallery Clo. NN3
Gallfield Ct. NN3
Gallowhill Rd. NN4
Gambrel Rd. NN5
Garfield Clo. NN2
Garfield St. NN2
Garners Way. NN7
Garrick Rd. NN1
Garsdale. NN2
Gas St. NN1
Gatelodge Clo. NN3
Gawaine Ct. NN3
Gayhurst Clo. NN3
Gedling Clo. NN3
George Nutt Ct. NN4
George Row. NN1
Georges Av. NN7
Georges Clo. NN7
Gervase Sq. NN3
Gibbsacre Ct.NN3
Gibson La. NN5
Gillsway. NN2
Glade Clo. NN3
Gladstone Rd.NN5
Glaisdale Clo. NN2
Glasgow St. NN5
Glassthorpe La. NN7
Glastonbury Rd. NN4
Glebe Av. NN4
Glebe Clo. NN4
Glebe La. NN4
Glebe Rd. NN7
Glebe Way. NN4
Glebe Way. NN7
Glebeland Cres.NN5
Glebeland Gdns. NN5
Glebeland Rd. NN5
Glebeland Wk. NN5
Glendale Ct. NN3
Glendock Rd. NN3
Glenfield Dri. NN29
Glenville. NN3
Gloucester Av. NN4
Gloucester Clo. NN4
Gloucester Clo. NN7
Gloucester Cres. NN4
Godwin Wk. NN5
Gold St. NN1
Goldcrest Ct. NN3
Goldenash Ct. NN3
Goldings Rd. NN3

wood Av. NN3 7 F5
on St. NN2 12 C4
e Clo. NN2 6 C4
erton Rd. NN4 18 B5
on Pl. NN1 5 B1
on St. NN1 5 A1
on Vw. NN4 22 A5
on Way. NN5 10 D2
ary Rd. NN4 21 F2
ge Av. NN5 10 D3
ge Clo. NN6 4 A2
ge Rd. NN3 8 A6
gefield. NN6 4 A2
gewood. NN4 20 D1
oin La. NN3 14 B3
scroft. NN2 6 A5
smere Av. NN3 14 C1
Clo. NN6 4 C3
St. NN1 13 E4
t Billing Way. NN3 9 F4
t Field Ct. NN3 8 D4
t Gull Cres. NN3 8 D3
t Holme Ct. NN3 8 C4
t La. NN7 25 D4
t Russell St. NN1 13 E4
tmeadow. NN3 9 F5
tmeadow Rd. NN3 9 F5
n End. NN2 12 C1
n La,
elfleys. NN4 16 B5
n La,
otton. NN4 22 A6
n Rd. NN7 23 B6
n St. NN1 5 A3
n St. NN7 20 B4
ndale Sq. NN3 15 G2
nfield Av. NN3 7 G6
nfield Rd. NN3 13 H1
nfinch Dri. NN3 8 A3
nglades. NN4 16 B4
nhills Clo. NN2 6 C3
nhills Rd. NN2 6 B3
enside,
uttermere Clo. NN3 8 B6
nview Dri. NN2 13 F1
nway. NN3 14 B3
nway Av. NN3 8 B5
nwood Clo. NN3 22 A3
nwood Rd.NN5 12 B5
ves Clo. NN5 10 C3
ory St. NN1 5 B3
don Wk. NN3 7 G5
ham Dri. NN4 16 B4
ille Av. NN3 7 H5
ille Clo NN2 6 D1
friars. NN1 5 C2
svenor Gdns. NN2 7 E5
undwell Ct. NN3 14 D2
ve La. NN3 22 B1
ve Rd. NN1 13 E4
ve Rd. NN7 23 A5
vebury Dell. NN2 6 B5
dhall Rd. NN1 5 D3
ston Rise. NN3 9 G5

es Rd. NN4 17 F2
Clo. NN5 11 E6
Clo, Harpole. NN7 24 B2
Clo,
slingbury. NN7 24 D4
am Clo. NN3 7 H2
piece Clo.NN3 9 G6
vell Ct. NN3 8 C5
Meadow Dri. NN3 15 G1
bledon Rise. NN4 16 C3
nlet Grn. NN5 11 H4
nmerstone La. NN4 16 C3
npton St. NN1 12 C4
nsterley Pk. NN3 9 E3
dley Clo. NN5 10 C3
emill Ct. NN3 15 G2
gerfield Ct. NN3 8 D6
borough Rd. NN2 6 C4
borough Rd Nth.
N2 6 C1
court Sq. NN6 4 B3
court Way. NN4 16 B3
ding Ter. NN1 12 C4
dingstone La. NN4 17 G5
dlands Rd. NN5 11 E4
dwater Rd. NN29 4 F2
dwick Rd. NN4 17 F6
dy Dri. NN4 22 A4
ebell Sq. NN3 15 G1
efield Rd. NN3 9 F4

Harefoot Clo. NN5 10 D3
Harlestone Rd,
New Duston. NN5 10 D1
Harlestone Rd,
Northampton. NN5 12 B5
Harmans Way. NN7 26 B2
Harold St. NN1 5 F2
Harrier Pk. NN4 17 E6
Harris Clo. NN4 22 A4
Harrow Way. NN2 6 A4
Harrowden Rd. NN4 18 C4
Harrowick La. NN6 4 A2
Hartburn Clo. NN3 15 G3
Hartwell Clo. NN2 7 E4
Harvest Way. NN2 6 A4
Harvey La. NN3 22 A3
Harvey Reeves Rd. NN5 16 D1
*Haselrig Sq,
Archangel Rd. NN4 16 C3
Hassocks Hedge. NN4 16 A4
Hatfield Clo. NN4 17 F6
Hatton Clo. NN3 7 G3
Haven Clo. NN5 12 B4
Hawkridge. NN4 16 C5
*Hawksbeard Pl,
Blueberry Rise. NN3 15 G1
Hawksmoor Way. NN5 11 F3
Hawksnet NN4 16 D6
Hawkstone Clo. NN5 11 F5
Hawthorn Rd. NN3 13 H2
Haycroft Way. NN2 6 B4
Haydown Grn.NN5 11 F3
Hayeswood Rd. NN3 8 D5
Hazeldene Rd. NN2 7 F6
Hazelwood Rd. NN1 5 E3
Healey Clo. NN3 9 G5
Heather La.NN3 8 C5
Heatherdale Way. NN2 7 F6
Heathfield Way. NN5 12 B2
Heathville. NN5 11 H3
Hedge End. NN4 21 F2
Hedge Way. NN4 21 F2
Hedgely Ct. NN4 16 D4
Hedgerow Dri. NN2 6 B4
Hellidon Clo. NN2 7 E5
Helmdon Cres. NN2 6 D5
Helmdon Rd. NN2 6 D5
Hembury Pl. NN4 16 C2
Henry St. NN1 13 F4
Herbert St. NN1 5 B2
Hereward Rd. NN4 17 E4
Hermitage Way. NN4 21 G2
Hern Hill Ct. NN4 16 B3
Heronsford. NN4 16 B6
Hertford Ct. NN3 15 E2
Hervey Clo. NN3 14 B2
Hester St. NN2 12 D4
Hexham Ct. NN4 16 D4
Heyford Rd. NN7 25 C2
Hidcote Rd. NN4 21 F1
Higgins Sq. NN4 16 C4
High Grn. NN4 22 C5
High St,
Bugbrooke. NN7 25 E3
High St,
Collingtree. NN4 21 F4
High St,
Earls Barton. NN6 4 B3
High St, Flore. NN7 26 E1
High St,
Great Billing. NN3 15 G1
High St,
Great Houghton. NN4 19 F3
High St,
Hardingstone. NN4 17 H5
High St,
Harpole. NN7 24 B2
High St,
Kingsthorpe. NN2 6 C6
High St,
Kislingbury. NN7 24 D4
High St,
Milton Malsor. NN7 20 B5
High St, Moulton. NN3 22 B2
High St,
Weedon Bec. NN7 26 B2
High St,
Weston Favell. NN3 14 B3
High St, Wootton. NN4 22 A5
High View. NN4 21 G2
Highdown Clo. NN4 16 B3
Highfield Rd. NN1 13 G2
Highlands Av. NN3 7 G5
Hilberry Rise. NN3 9 H5
Hill Clo. NN5 11 E2

Hill Farm Rise. NN4 16 D6
Hillcrest Av. NN3 7 H6
Hilldrop Rd. NN4 17 E6
Hillside Cres. NN7 25 B2
Hillside Rd, Flore. NN7 26 D1
Hillside Rd,
Nether Heyford. NN7 25 A2
Hillside Way. NN3 14 A3
Hinton Clo. NN2 6 C4
Hinton Rd. NN2 6 C4
Hirondelle Clo. NN5 10 C3
Hobby Clo. NN4 17 E6
Hocknell Clo. NN4 22 B5
Hodges La. NN7 24 D5
Holbein Gdns. NN4 16 C6
Holcutt Clo. NN4 22 B1
Holdenby Rd. NN2 7 E5
Hollingside Dri. NN2 7 F6
Hollow Bank. NN3 8 B3
Holly Lodge Dri. NN2 6 C4
Holly Rd. NN1 13 F3
Holman Clo. NN3 14 B2
Holmecross Rd. NN3 8 C4
Holmfield Way NN3 14 A3
Holmleigh Clo.NN5 11 E5
Holmwood Clo. NN5 10 C3
Holyrood Rd. NN5 11 H5
Home Farm Clo. NN3 15 F3
Homestead Clo. NN3 22 C2
Homestead Dri. NN7 25 F3
Homestead Rise. NN4 21 G2
Homestead Way. NN2 13 E2
Honeysuckle Way. NN3 14 A6
Honister Grn. NN3 8 A6
Hood St. NN1 13 E4
Hopmeadow Ct. NN3 9 F5
Hopping Hill Gdns. NN5 11 F3
Hornbeam Ct. NN3 8 C6
Hornby Rd. NN6 4 B2
Horse Market. NN1 5 B3
Horse Shoe St. NN1 5 B3
Horsemoor Sq. NN3 15 G1
Horsewell Ct. NN3 8 A2
Horsley Rd. NN2 12 C2
Horton Rd. NN7 23 A6
Houghton Hill. NN4 18 A5
*Howard Billy Gdns,
Buttermere Clo. NN3 8 B6
Howard La. NN2 6 C2
Hoxton Clo. NN3 8 C3
Hoylake Dri. NN2 7 F6
Hudson Dri. NN4 16 B5
Humber Clo. NN5 11 H2
Humfrey La. NN2 6 D1
Hunsbarrow Rd. NN4 16 B2
Hunsbury Clo.NN4 16 C5
Hunsbury Grn. NN4 16 B4
Hunsbury Hill Av. NN4 16 B3
Hunsbury Hill Rd. NN4 16 B4
Hunslet La. NN4 16 B4
Hunter St. NN1 13 E4
Hunters Clo. NN2 6 D3
Huntsham Clo. NN3 14 B4
Huntsmead. NN3 9 H5
Huxloe Rise. NN3 8 C3
Hybiscus Clo. NN3 14 A5

Ibstock Clo. NN3 9 E3
Icknield Dri. NN4 16 C5
Ilex Clo. NN4 18 A5
INDUSTRIAL ESTATES:
Brackmills Business Pk.
NN4 18 B4
Brackmills Ind Est.
NN4 18 C3
Cavalry Hill Ind Est.
NN7 26 A2
Cornwall Business Pk.
NN4 18 C4
Grosvenor Shopping
Centre. NN1 5 D2
Lodge Farm Ind Est.
NN1 11 E1
Moulton Pk Ind Est.
NN3 7 G3
Northampton Business
Pk. NN4 18 A5
Peacock Place. NN1 5 D2
Riverside Retail Pk.
NN3 14 C5
St Peters Way Shopping
Centre. NN1 5 C3
Weston Favell Shopping
Centre. NN3 14 D1
Ingleborough Way. NN5 11 F3

Inglewood Ct. NN3 15 G2
Irondale Clo. NN4 16 B2
Ironstone La. NN4 16 B3
Isham Clo. NN2 7 E4
Ivy Rd. NN1 13 F3
Ixworth Clo. NN3 9 E4

Jackdaw Clo. NN3 15 G3
James Lewis Ct. NN3 14 B1
Jardine Clo. NN3 14 C2
Jasmine Rd. NN3 9 G4
Javelin Clo. NN5 11 E4
Jenner Cres. NN2 6 C4
Jersey Ct. NN3 14 D2
Jeyes Clo. NN3 22 A2
John Gray Rd. NN29 4 F1
Johns Rd. NN7 25 F3
Joshua Sq. NN4 16 C4
Jubilee Clo. NN4 16 C3
Julian Way. NN2 6 B6
Junction Rd. NN2 13 F2
Juniper Ct. NN3 9 G6

Kealdale Rd. NN3 7 G5
Keats Clo. NN4 19 F4
Keats Clo. NN6 4 C3
Kedlestone Clo. NN4 17 F6
Kelburn Clo. NN4 21 E1
Kelmscott Clo. NN3 9 E4
Kelsall Clo. NN5 10 D4
Kendal Clo. NN3 8 B5
Kenilworth Clo. NN5 11 E4
Kenmuir Av. NN2 13 F1
Kenmuir Cres. NN2 13 F1
Kenmuir Gdns. NN2 13 G1
Kennet Gdns. NN5 11 H2
Kent Clo. NN5 11 E6
Kent Rd. NN5 11 E6
Kentford Clo. NN4 17 E5
Kentstone Clo. NN2 6 A5
Kerrfield Est. NN5 11 E4
Kestrel Clo. NN3 14 C2
Keswick Dri. NN3 8 A5
Kettering Rd. NN1 13 E5
Kettering Rd. NN3 22 D2
Kettering Rd Nth. NN3 8 A5
Keyham Ct. NN3 9 E4
Kilvey Rd. NN4 18 B4
Kimble Clo. NN4 17 E6
King Edward St. NN1 13 G5
King St. NN1 5 C2
King St. NN6 4 B2
Kingfisher Clo. NN4 20 D1
Kingmaker Way. NN4 16 D4
Kings La. NN7 26 F2
Kings Pk. NN7 26 B3
Kings Pk Rd. NN3 7 F3
Kingscroft Ct. NN3 15 F2
Kingsfield Clo. NN5 12 A2
Kingsfield Way. NN5 12 A2
Kingsland Av. NN2 6 D6
Kingsland Clo. NN2 7 E6
Kingsland Gdns. NN2 6 D6
Kingsley Gdns. NN2 13 E2
Kingsley Rd. NN2 13 E2
Kingsmead. NN2 6 B4
Kingsthorpe Gro. NN2 12 D1
Kingsthorpe Rd. NN2 12 D1
Kingsway. NN2 6 B5
Kingswell Rd. NN2 12 C1
Kingswell St. NN1 5 C3
Kinross Clo. NN3 7 G5
Kirby Clo. NN4 22 B5
Kirton Clo. NN3 9 F5
Kislingbury Rd. NN7 25 E3
Kites Clo. NN4 16 D6
Knaphill Cres. NN4 16 C2
Knightle Rd. NN2 12 C3
Knighton Clo. NN5 10 D1
Knights Clo. NN6 4 B2
Knights Ct. NN3 15 F3
Knights La. NN2 6 B6
Knightscliffe Way. NN5 11 F3
Knowle Clo. NN3 14 A5
Kyoto Clo. NN3 7 G3

Laburnum Cres. NN3 13 G1
Lady Hollows Dri. NN4 22 C5
Lady Winefrides Wk.
NN3 15 F1
Ladybridge Dri.NN4 16 A5
Ladys La. NN1 5 C2
Lake Walk. NN4 21 F4
Lakeside Dri. NN3 9 H6
Lakeside Hollow. NN4 21 F3

Lancaster Way. NN4 16 D4
Lancelot Ct. NN5 10 D4
Lancers Way. NN7 26 B2
Lancing Clo. NN4 16 A5
Landcross Dri. NN3 14 A4
Lanercost Wk. NN3 8 B5
Langdale Rd. NN2 12 D1
Langford Dri. NN4 21 G3
Langley Clo. NN4 16 B3
Langsett Clo. NN3 14 D2
Lansdown Dri. NN3 14 C1
Lapwing Clo. NN4 20 D1
Larch La. NN5 10 D2
Lark Rise. NN3 9 E5
Larkhall La. NN7 24 B2
Larkhall Way. NN7 24 C1
Larwood Clo. NN2 6 A4
Lasham Ct. NN3 15 G2
Latymer Ct. NN1 5 C2
Lauderdale Av. NN4 16 D3
Laurel Ct. NN3 8 C6
Laurel Valley. NN4 21 G4
Lavant Wk. NN3 7 F5
Lavenham Clo. NN3 8 D4
Lawrence Ct. NN1 12 D4
Lawson Cres. NN3 15 G2
Lea Rd. NN1 13 G3
Leafields. NN3 14 D3
Leah Bank. NN4 16 D3
Leben Sq. NN3 9 G4
Ledaig Way. NN3 7 G5
Leicester St. NN1 12 D4
Leith Ct. NN4 16 B3
Lennox Wk. NN5 11 F2
Leslie Rd. NN2 12 C4
Letts Rd. NN4 17 E2
Levitts Rd. NN7 25 F3
Lewis Rd. NN5 12 A4
Lexden Clo. NN4 22 B4
Leyland Dri. NN2 6 A4
Leys La. NN4 19 F4
Leys Rd. NN6 4 A3
Leyside Ct. NN3 9 F4
Leyswell Ct. NN3 15 E4
Liberty Dri. NN5 11 E3
Lichfield Clo. NN7 24 D5
Lichfield Dri. NN4 21 E1
Liddington Way. NN2 6 C4
Liliput Rd. NN4 18 C3
Lime Av. NN3 13 H3
Lime Farm Way. NN4 19 F4
Lime Gro. NN7 25 F3
Limefields Way. NN4 21 G2
Limehurst Clo. NN5 11 E3
Limlow Clo. NN4 16 B3
Limoges Ct. NN5 10 C2
Linacre Clo. NN3 8 D3
Lincoln Rd. NN5 12 B6
Lincoln St. NN2 6 C6
Lindale Clo. NN3 7 H6
Linden Rd. NN3 13 G2
Lindisfarne Way. NN4 17 F6
Lindsay Av. NN3 13 G2
Lindsay Ter. NN3 13 H1
Lings Way. NN3 9 E4
Lingswood Pk. NN3 9 E6
Link Rd. NN2 6 B3
Linley Grn. NN5 11 F4
Lismore Clo. NN3 15 G1
Lister Dri. NN4 16 B5
Little Billing Way. NN3 15 E1
Little Cross St. NN1 5 B2
Little Gull Clo. NN3 8 D3
Little La. NN4 19 F3
Little Priel Rd. NN7 26 C2
Littleton Rd. NN5 12 B4
Littlewood Clo. NN5 12 B5
Loire Clo. NN5 10 C1
Lockcroft Sq. NN3 15 H1
Lockwood Clo. NN2 6 D5
Lodge Av. NN4 21 F4
Lodge Clo. NN5 11 E3
Lodge Clo. NN7 19 H2
Lodge Rd. NN7 19 H2
Lodge Way. NN5 10 D1
Lodore Gdns. NN3 8 A6
Logwell Ct. NN3 14 D3
Lombardy Ct. NN3 8 C6
London End. NN6 4 A3
London Rd. NN4 17 F5
Long Acres. NN4 17 E6
Long Mallow Rise. NN3 15 G2
Long Marsh Sq. NN3 9 E3
Long Meadow. NN4 22 C5
Long Mynd Dri. NN5 11 F4

Longford Av. NN3 15 E4
Longland Ct. NN3 14 A1
Longland Rd. NN3 14 A1
Longleat Ct. NN4 17 F6
Longmead Ct. NN3 9 F5
Longueville Ct. NN3 8 C5
Lordswood Clo. NN4 22 B5
Lorne Rd. NN1 12 D4
Lorraine Cres. NN3 8 A4
Lorraine Dri.NN3 8 A4
Louise Rd. NN1 12 D4
Lovat Cameron Dri. NN5 11 G5
Low Farm Pl. NN3 7 F2
Low Grn. NN4 22 C5
Lowbury Ct. NN4 16 B2
Lower Adelaide St. NN2 12 C4
Lower Bath St. NN1 5 A2
Lower Cross St. NN1 5 B2
Lower Farm Rd. NN3 7 F2
Lower Harding St. NN1 5 B1
Lower Hester St. NN2 12 C4
Lower Meadow Ct. NN3 8 D4
Lower Mounts. NN1 5 E2
Lower Priory St. NN1 12 C4
Lower Rd. NN7 20 C4
Lower Thrift St. NN1 13 F5
Lowick Ct. NN3 8 A2
Lowlands Clo. NN3 9 G4
Loxton Clo. NN5 11 E3
Loyd Rd. NN1 13 G4
Lucast Ct. NN3 8 A2
Ludlow Clo. NN3 9 E3
Lumbertubs La.NN3 8 B4
Lumbertubs Rise. NN3 8 B4
Lumbertubs Way. NN3 8 B3
Lunchfield Ct. NN3 22 B2
Lunchfield Gdns. NN3 22 B2
Lunchfield La. NN3 22 B2
Lunchfield Wk. NN3 22 B2
Lutterworth Rd. NN1 13 G4
Lyncrest Av. NN5 11 G5
Lyncroft Way. NN2 12 C2
Lynmouth Av. NN3 14 A5
Lynton Av. NN2 6 C3
Lytham Clo. NN2 7 F6
Lyveden Rd. NN4 18 C4

Maclean Clo. NN3 14 A4
Macmillan Way. NN3 8 A5
Macon Clo. NN5 10 C2
Magee St. NN1 13 F4
Magnolia Clo. NN3 14 B5
Maidencastle. NN3 9 F6
Main Rd. NN4 17 E2
Main Rd. NN5 10 D2
Main Rd. NN6 4 A1
Malcolm Dri. NN5 11 G5
Malcolm Rd. NN2 13 G2
Malcolm Ter. NN2 13 G1
Mallard Clo. NN4 16 C4
Mallard Clo. NN6 4 B2
Mallory Wk. NN3 7 F4
Malpas Dr. NN5 10 D4
Malvern Gro.NN5 11 F4
Malzor La. NN7 20 B4
Manfield Rd. NN1 13 G4
Manfield Way. NN3 7 H5
Manning Ct. NN3 8 A2
Manning Rd.NN3 8 A2
Mannington Gdns. NN4 21 F1
Manock Sq. NN4 16 C4
Manor Clo. NN7 24 C2
Manor Farm Rd. NN3 15 F1
Manor House Ct. NN6 4 B2
Manor Pk. NN7 25 B1
Manor Rd. NN2 6 C6
Manor Rd. NN3 22 A3
Manor Rd. NN6 4 A2
Manor Rd. NN6 4 B2
Manor Rd. NN7 26 B3
Manor Wk. NN7 25 B1
Manorfield Clo. NN3 15 F3
Manorfield Rd. NN3 15 E4
Mansard Clo. NN5 11 G6
Mansion Clo. NN3 7 G3
Maple Clo. NN7 25 E4
Mapperley Av. NN3 14 D3
Marchwood Clo. NN3 8 D4
Mare Fair. NN1 5 B3
Margaret St. NN1 5 D1
Market Sq. NN1 5 C3
Market St. NN1 13 F4
Markham Clo. NN5 11 F3
Marlborough Rd. NN5 12 B6

Marlowe Clo. NN4 21 E1
Marlstones NN4 16 B4
Marquee Dri. NN3 14 D4
Marriott St. NN2 12 D3
Marseilles Clo. NN5 10 C2
Marshleys Ct. NN3 9 F4
Marshwell Ct. NN3 15 E4
Martel Clo. NN5 10 B3
Martindale. NN2 6 A4
Martins La. NN4 17 G5
Martins Yd. NN5 12 C5
Marwood Clo. NN3 14 A5
Masefield Way. NN2 13 E2
Massey Clo.NN4 17 H6
Masters Ct. NN4 21 F2
Matchless Clo. NN5 10 C3
Mayfield Rd. NN3 13 H1
Meadow Clo. NN5 10 D2
Meadow Farm Clo. NN1 26 F2
Meadow La. NN7 19 H2
Meadow Vw. NN2 6 A4
Meadway. NN3 14 B3
Meadway. NN7 25 E4
Medbourne Clo. NN3 7 H2
Medellin Hill. NN3 8 D3
Medinah Clo. NN4 21 F3
Medway Dri. NN5 11 G2
Meeting La. NN5 11 E5
Melbourne La. NN5 11 E5
Melbourne St. NN1 13 F5
Melbourne St.NN5 12 A5
Melbury La. NN3 9 F6
Melbury Pl. NN3 9 E6
Melchester Clo. NN4 22 A4
Meldon Clo. NN4 17 F6
Melrose Av. NN5 11 G4
Meltham Clo. NN3 14 D2
Melville St. NN1 13 F5
Mendip Rd. NN5 11 F5
Meon Way. NN5 11 F4
Mercers Row. NN1 5 C3
Mercia Clo. NN3 14 A2
Mercury Dri. NN4 18 B3
Mere Clo. NN4 17 E5
Mere Clo. NN7 23 B6
Mere Way. NN4 17 E5
Merlin Gro. NN4 17 E6
Merry Hill. NN4 16 B3
Merrydale St. NN3 9 E3
Mershe Clo. NN4 22 A4
Merthyr Rd. NN5 12 A3
Meshaw Cres. NN3 14 A4
Micklewell La. NN3 9 E3
Middle Greeve. NN4 22 C5
Middle March. NN3 9 F5
Middle Mead Ct. NN3 15 E2
Middle St. NN7 25 B1
Middlemore. NN3 8 D3
Middleton Clo. NN2 6 D4
Middlewell Ct. NN3 14 D3
Midfield Ct. NN3 8 D4
Milbury. NN6 4 C3
Miles Well Ct. NN3 8 C6
Military Rd. NN1 13 E4
Mill La. NN2 12 C4
Mill La. NN5 12 A3
Mill La. NN6 4 C3
Mill La, Cogenhoe. NN7 23 D1
Mill La, Kislingbury. NN7 24 C5
Mill Meadow. NN2 6 D5
Mill Rd. NN2 12 C4
Mill Rd. NN7 24 C5
Millbank. NN3 15 H1
Millbrook Clo. NN5 16 D1
Miller Hill. NN4 16 C4
Millers Clo. NN7 24 C6
Mills Clo. NN6 4 B3
Millside Clo. NN2 7 E4
Millstone Clo. NN4 16 A4
Millway. NN5 11 E5
Milton Bri. NN4 22 C5
Milton Ct. NN7 20 B5
Milton St. NN2 13 F2
Milton St Nth. NN2 13 E2
Milverton Cres. NN3 14 B4
Mitchell Clo. NN5 11 F2
Moat Pl. NN1 5 A2
Monarch Rd. NN2 12 D3
Monks Hill Rd. NN1 13 G4
Monks Pk Rd. NN1 13 G4
Monks Pond St. NN1 5 A1
Monmouth Rd. NN5 12 B4

Montague Cres. NN5 11 F2
Montfort Clo. NN5 11 G5
Moore St. NN2 13 F2
Moores Clo. NN7 25 E4
Moorfield Sq. NN3 9 E3
Moorland Clo. NN3 14 C1
Mordaunt La. NN5 11 F2
Moreton Way. NN2 6 C4
Morgan Clo. NN3 9 G5
Morris Rd. NN2 6 D6
Mortar Pit Rd. NN3 9 G4
Mortimer Clo. NN4 16 D4
Mortons Bush. NN4 22 B5
Motspur Dri. NN2 12 C2
Moulton La. NN2 6 D1
Moulton Way. NN3 8 A3
Moulton Way Nth. NN3 8 A3
Moulton Way Sth. NN3 8 A3
Mount Pleasant. NN6 4 B3
Mountclair Ct. NN3 14 C3
Mountfield Rd. NN3 7 G6
Mounts Ct. NN3 8 C6
Mulberry Clo. NN5 11 H5
Muncaster Gdns. NN4 21 G1
Murry Av. NN2 13 E2
Muscott Clo. NN7 26 E1
Muscott La. NN5 11 E5
Muscott St. NN5 12 B5
Museum Way. NN3 14 D5
Musgrave Clo. NN4 22 B5
Mushroom Rd. NN3 15 G1

Naomi Clo. NN3 14 D3
Naseby St. NN2 12 C3
Navigation Row. NN1 17 F1
Neale Clo. NN3 14 C3
Nene Dri. NN5 11 H1
Nene Rise. NN7 23 C2
Nene Side Clo. NN7 26 B3
Nene Valley Way. NN3 14 A6
Nene Valley Way.NN4 18 A4
Nene Wk. NN5 11 H1
Nene Way. NN5 12 A1
Nene Way. NN7 24 C5
Nesbitt Clo. NN3 14 C4
Nether Jackson Ct. NN3 9 F5
Nether La. NN7 26 F2
Nethermead Ct. NN3 8 D5
Nettle Gap Clo. NN4 22 B5
New Croft. NN7 26 B4
New Rd. NN4 22 A5
New St. NN6 4 B3
New St. NN7 26 C4
Newby Ct. NN3 8 A6
Newcombe Rd. NN5 12 B5
Newington Rd. NN2 6 D5
Newland. NN1 5 C1
Newlands Sq. NN2 6 D5
Newnham Rd. NN2 7 E6
Newport Pagnell Rd. NN4 22 A4
Newport Rd. NN5 12 B4
Newstead Clo. NN3 9 G6
Newstone Cres. NN4 16 C2
Newton Rd.NN5 11 E3
Nicholls Ct. NN3 8 C4
Norfolk St. NN2 12 C3
Norfolk Ter. NN2 12 C3
Norman D Gate. NN1 17 H1
Norman Rd. NN3 14 A2
Normead Sq. NN3 15 H1
North Hayes Ct. NN3 8 D4
North Holme Ct. NN3 8 C4
North Leys Ct. NN3 8 A2
North Oval. NN5 11 H2
North Paddock Ct. NN3 8 D5
North Portway Clo. NN3 8 D2
North Priors Ct. NN3 9 E5
North Rd. NN6 4 B2
North Western Av. NN2 6 B5
Northampton La. NN3 22 B3
Northampton La Sth. NN3 8 A3
Northampton Rd. NN6 4 A2
Northampton Rd, Blisworth. NN7 20 B6
Northampton Rd, Harpole. NN7 24 C3
Northcote St. NN2 12 C4
Northfield Rd. NN5 11 E3
Northfield Way.NN2 6 C5
Northumbria Gdns. NN3 14 A2
Northwood Rd. NN3 13 H2
Norton Rd. NN2 6 D6

Notre Dame Mews. NN1 5 E2
Nunns Mill Rd. NN1 17 H1
Nursery La. NN2 6 D6
Nuthall Clo. NN3 14 D3

Oak Park Clo. NN3 9 E3
Oak St. NN1 12 D4
Oak St. NN7 26 A4
Oakgrove Pl. NN4 21 G2
Oakham Clo. NN3 7 H3
Oaklands Dri. NN3 14 C2
Oaklands, Bugbrooke. NN7 25 F4
Oaklands, Weedon. NN7 26 A4
Oakleigh Dri. NN5 11 E3
Oakley Dri. NN3 22 B2
Oakley St. NN1 13 E4
Oakmont Clo. NN4 21 F3
Oakwood Rd. NN1 13 G2
Oat Hill Dri. NN3 15 G2
Obelisk Clo. NN2 6 D2
Obelisk Rise. NN2 6 D2
Old Barn Ct. NN3 9 E5
Old Quarry Ct. NN3 8 C5
Old Towcester Rd. NN4 17 F2
Old Yew Ct. NN2 6 C6
Olden Rd. NN3 9 G4
Oldenmead Ct. NN3 8 D6
Oleander Cres. NN3 9 G5
Olympia Clo. NN4 17 E6
Oransay Clo. NN3 15 G1
Orchard Clo. NN4 22 A5
Orchard Clo. NN7 20 C4
Orchard Grn. NN3 14 B2
Orchard Hill. NN3 15 E2
Orchard St. NN5 12 B5
Orchard Way. NN5 11 E5
Orchard Way, Cogenhoe. NN7 23 C2
Orchard Way, Harpole. NN7 24 B2
Ordnance Rd. NN7 26 A2
Osbourne Jetty. NN1 5 C3
Osbourne Rd. NN2 12 D1
Osler Clo. NN2 6 C4
Osmond Dri. NN3 9 E4
Osprey Rise. NN4 17 E6
Osyth Clo. NN4 18 C3
Oulton Rise. NN3 7 G5
Oundle Dri. NN3 7 H3
Overleys Ct. NN3 9 F4
Overmead Rd. NN3 15 G1
Overslade. NN4 16 D5
Overstone Clo. NN3 22 C2
Overstone La, Moulton. NN3 22 D2
Overstone La, Overstone. NN3 9 F4
Overstone Rd. NN1 5 E1
Overstone Rd.NN3 22 B3
Owen Ct. NN7 23 B5
Owl Clo. NN3 7 F2
Oxburgh Ct. NN4 17 F6
Oxford Clo. NN6 4 C3
Oxford St. NN4 17 E3
Oxwich Clo. NN4 18 B4

Paddock Mill Ct. NN3 9 F5
Paddock Way. NN3 15 E2
Padwell Ct. NN3 15 E4
Paget Clo. NN4 19 F4
Palmer Sq. NN3 15 G3
Palmerston Rd. NN1 13 F5
Parade Bank. NN3 22 B2
Park Av. NN5 10 D3
Park Av Nth. NN3 13 G1
Park Av Sth. NN3 13 H3
Park Clo. NN5 10 D3
Park Clo. NN6 4 A3
Park Clo. NN7 23 B6
Park Cres East. NN5 11 H2
Park Cres West. NN5 11 H2
Park Dri. NN5 11 H2
Park Hill Rd. NN3 8 C6
Park La. NN5 10 C3
Park La. NN6 4 A3
Park La. NN7 24 B2
Park Sq. NN5 11 H2
Park St. NN6 4 A3
Park View. NN3 22 C3
Park View Clo. NN3 22 D2
Park Wk. NN5 11 H2
Parkfield Av. NN4 17 F5
Parkfield Cres. NN4 17 F4

Parklands Av. NN3
Parklands Cres. NN3
Parkside. NN3
Parkway. NN3
Parkwood St. NN5
Parracombe Way. NN3
Parsons Clo. NN7
Parsons Meads. NN4
Partridge Clo. NN2
Parva Ct. NN3
Pasteur Clo. NN2
Patterson Clo. NN3
Pavilion Dri. NN4
Paxton Rd. NN3
Peace Hill. NN7
Peace Pl. NN4
Pearmain Ct. NN3
Peartree Clo. NN3
Pelham Ct. NN3
Pell Ct. NN3
Pembroke Cres. NN5
Pembroke Gdns.NN5
Pembroke Rd. NN5
Pen Ct. NN1
Penarth Rd. NN5
Pendle Rd. NN5
Penfold Dri. NN3
Penfold Gdns. NN3
Penfold La. NN3
Peniston Rd. NN3
Penn Gdns. NN4
Pennard Clo. NN4
Pennine Way. NN5
Pennycress Pl. NN3
Penrhyn Rd. NN4
Penvale Rd. NN4
Peppercorn Way. NN4
Percival Clo. NN5
Percy Rd. NN1
Peregrine Pl. NN4
Perry St. NN1
Peverels Way. NN5
Peveril Rd. NN5
Pheasant Way. NN2
Piccadilly Clo. NN4
Pike La. NN1
Pikemead Ct. NN3
Pilgrims La. NN7
Pilgrims Pl. NN4
Pilton Clo. NN3
Pine Copse Clo. NN5
Pine Ridge. NN3
Pine Trees. NN3
Pineham Av. NN2
Pinewood Rd. NN3
Pippin Clo. NN7
Pippin La. NN3
Pitsford Rd. NN3
Pitstone Rd. NN4
Plantagenet Sq. NN4
Pleydell Gdns. NN4
Pleydell Rd. NN4
Plough La. NN2
Ploughmans Wk. NN2
Poachers Way. NN2
Poitiers Ct. NN5
Pond Farm Clo. NN5
Poole St. NN1
Poplar Ct. NN3
Poppyfield Ct. NN3
Porlock Clo. NN5
Port Rd. NN5
Portland Pl. NN1
Portstone Clo. NN5
Pound La. NN3
Pound La. NN3
Pound La. NN7
Poyntz Gdns. NN5
Poyntz La. NN5
Prentice Ct. NN3
Prescott Clo. NN3
Prestbury Rd. NN5
Preston Ct. NN3
Prestwold Way. NN3
Primula Clo. NN3
Prince of Wales Row. NN3
Prince St. NN6
Princes Clo. NN7
Princess Clo. NN3
Priory Clo. NN3
Pritchard Clo. NN3
Probyn Clo. NN3
Provence Ct. NN5
Purser Rd. NN1

le Way. NN4 20 D1
Way. NN3 14 C3
ley St. NN1 5 F2
ley Vw. NN3 22 B2
ley Way. NN5 10 D2

ers Clo. NN7 25 E4
tock Cres. NN5 11 F4
y Park Clo. NN3 7 H3
y Rd. NN5 10 D2
erstone. NN4 16 A4
ec Rd. NN4 21 H1
n Eleanor Rd. NN4 17 E3
n Eleanor Ter. NN4 17 F4
n St. NN6 4 B2
n St. NN7 26 A4
ns Gdns. NN2 12 D1
ns Pk. NN7 26 B3
ns Rd. NN1 13 E4
nswood Av. NN3 8 B5
nstone La. NN4 16 C3
on Rd. NN4 22 A6
n Way. NN1 5 A1

igh Clo. NN4 16 D3
one Way. NN2 6 D4
urn Rd. NN2 13 F1
urn Ter. NN2 13 F1
n St. NN1 5 F1
borough Cres.
4 16 C2
s Field Clo. NN3 9 G6
tone Clo. NN4 21 G2
all Rd. NN2 13 F2
me Rd. NN4 17 F2
ns Way. NN3 15 G3
nscroft. NN4 16 D6
y Cres. NN5 10 C3
ond Rd NN5 12 B4
sford Rd. NN5 12 A3
lo. NN4 21 E1
ry Farm Rd. NN3 9 G4
ry La. NN7 20 B5
House Wharf. NN7 26 C2
ouse Rd. NN3 7 F3
nd Dri. NN2 6 A5
th Clo. NN4 17 E4
ing Av. NN3 8 A3
ham Clo. NN5 11 E3
hill. NN4 16 B5
way. NN3 7 G5
ncy Clo. NN7 26 B2
nt Sq. NN1 5 C1
nt St. NN1 5 B1
s Ct. NN5 10 C2
shaw Way. NN2 7 F6
n Ct. NN3 8 B5
aven Rd.NN4 21 G2
d Clo. NN3 8 D5
ard Way. NN2 6 D3
li Rd. NN4 18 B4
e Clo. NN5 11 H1
nond Ter. NN5 12 B5
ard Rd. NN3 8 C6
Ct. NN3 8 A2
Wk. NN3 14 C3
walk Dri. NN3 9 G6
way. NN3 14 A3
Clo. NN3 9 G5
ood Ct. NN3 8 D5
Way. NN4 16 D2
wood Clo. NN2 6 B5
Clo. NN4 16 D3
side Ct,
ngbury. NN7 24 D4
side Ct,
edon. NN7 26 B3
side Dri. NN7 26 B3
side Way. NN1 17 H1
stone Way. NN4 16 A4
well. NN3 15 H1
Clo. NN3 14 D2
t St. NN1 5 D1
ts Field. NN7 25 A2
ia Clo. NN4 16 C2
nson Ho,
ather La. NN3 8 C5
elle Way. NN5 10 C2
roft Clo. NN4 21 G2
ngham Rd. NN4 17 F3
d. NN1 13 G3
y Wk. NN5 11 F3
Cres. NN7 25 A2
ny Rd. NN2 13 E2
ery La. NN2 6 B3

Roseberry Av. NN5 11 H5
Rosedale Rd. NN2 6 D6
Roseholme Rd. NN1 13 G4
Rosemoor Dri. NN4 21 F1
Rosenella Clo. NN4 16 C3
Rosgill Pl. NN3 14 A1
Ross Rd. NN5 11 G6
Rossette Clo. NN5 11 E4
Rothersthorpe Av. NN4 16 D3
Rothersthorpe Cres.
NN4 16 D3
Rothersthorpe La. NN4 16 D4
Rothersthorpe Rd. NN4 16 D3
Rothersthorpe Rd. NN7 24 D5
Rothesay Rd. NN2 13 F1
Rowan Av. NN3 8 B4
Rowandson Clo. NN3 14 C2
Rowtree Rd. NN4 20 C1
Ruddington Clo. NN3 14 C4
Rudge Mews. NN5 10 C3
Rufford Av. NN3 14 C4
Rushmere Av. NN1 13 H5
Rushmere Cres. NN3 14 A5
Rushmere Rd. NN1 18 B1
Rushmere Rd. NN3 14 A6
Rushmills. NN4 18 C2
Rushy End. NN4 21 E2
Ruskin Rd. NN2 6 D5
Russell Rise. NN1 26 E2
Russell Sq. NN3 8 A3
Russett Dri. NN3 15 E2
Rutland Way. NN3 7 H3
Rydal Mount. NN3 8 A6
Rydalside. NN4 16 C3
Ryehill Clo. NN5 11 E2
Ryehill Ct. NN5 11 F2
Ryehill Rd. NN3 8 D6
Ryland Rd. NN2 13 F2
Ryland Rd. NN3 22 A3
Ryland Rd. NN5 10 D3
Ryland Way. NN5 10 D3

Saddlebeck Rd. NN5 11 F6
Saddlers Sq. NN3 8 D3
Saffron Clo. NN4 21 G3
Sage Clo. NN3 8 C5
St Albans Rd. NN3 13 H1
St Andrews Rd. NN1 5 A2
St Andrews St. NN1 5 B1
St Benedicts Mnt. NN4 16 B4
St Crispin Rd. NN6 4 C3
St Davids Rd.NN2 12 D1
St Dunstans Rise. NN4 16 B4
St Edmunds Rd. NN1 5 F2
St Edmunds St. NN1 13 F5
St Emilion Clo. NN5 10 B3
St Francis Av. NN5 12 B3
St Georges Av. NN2 12 D3
St Georges St. NN1 12 C4
St Giles Sq. NN1 5 D3
St Giles St. NN1 5 D3
St Giles Ter. NN1 5 E2
St Gregory's Rd. NN3 8 B6
St James Mill Rd. NN5 12 B6
St James Park Rd. NN5 12 B5
St James Rd. NN5 12 B5
St James St. NN1 5 C4
St Johns Av. NN2 6 D3
St Johns St. NN1 5 D4
St Johns Ter. NN1 5 D4
St Julien Clo. NN5 10 C2
St Katherines St. NN1 5 B3
St Katherines Ter. NN1 5 B3
St Leonards Rd. NN4 17 F2
St Liz St. NN1 12 C4
St Margarets Gdns.
NN5 12 A2
St Marks Cres.NN2 6 B3
St Martins Clo. NN2 6 D5
St Martyns Way. NN7 26 B3
St Marys Rd. NN7 26 B3
St Marys St. NN1 5 B3
St Michaels Av. NN1 13 F4
St Michaels Mnt. NN1 13 F4
St Michaels Rd. NN1 5 E1
St Pauls Rd. NN2 12 D3
St Peters Gdns. NN3 14 C3
St Peters Sq. NN1 5 B4
St Peters St. NN1 5 B3
St Peters Walk. NN1 5 C3
St Peters Way. NN1 5 A3
St Peters Way,
Cogenhoe. NN7 23 C2
St Peters Way,
Weedon. NN7 26 B3

St Thomas Rd. NN7 23 A5
Salcey St. NN4 17 F3
Salisbury St. NN2 12 C4
Sallow Av. NN3 9 G6
Salthouse Rd. NN4 18 B3
Saltwell Sq. NN3 15 G1
Sanwell Way. NN4 16 A4
Sandfield Clo. NN3 7 H3
Sandhill St. NN5 12 A4
Sandhills Clo. NN2 6 C3
Sandhills Rd. NN2 6 C3
Sandhurst Clo. NN4 17 E5
Sandiland Rd. NN3 14 A1
Sandover. NN4 21 G2
Sandringham Clo. NN1 13 H5
Sandringham Rd. NN1 13 H4
Sandy Hill La.NN1 22 C2
Sandy La. NN5 10 B3
Sansom Ct. NN3 8 C6
Sarek Pk. NN4 16 C6
Sargeants La. NN4 21 F4
Saruman La. NN3 9 F4
Savill Clo. NN4 21 F2
Saxon Lodge. NN6 4 B3
Saxon Rise. NN5 11 E5
Saxon Rise. NN6 4 B3
Saxon St. NN3 14 A3
Scarletwell St. NN1 5 A2
School La,
Harpole. NN7 24 B2
School La,
Kislingbury. NN7 24 D5
Scirocco Clo. NN3 7 F3
Scotia Clo. NN4 18 D3
Scotney Clo. NN4 17 F5
Seagrave Ct. NN3 9 F4
Sears Clo. NN7 26 F1
Seaton Dri. NN3 14 D3
Sedgwick Clo. NN3 8 D6
Seedfield Clo. NN3 14 C3
Semilong Rd. NN2 12 D4
Sentinel Rd. NN4 16 B4
Severn Dri. NN5 11 H2
Seymour St. NN5 12 B5
Shadowfax Dri. NN3 9 F4
Shakespeare Rd. NN1 13 E4
Shale End. NN5 10 D1
Shard Clo. NN4 21 F2
Sharman Rd. NN5 12 B6
Sharrow Pl. NN3 15 H1
Shatterstone. NN4 21 G2
Sheaf Clo. NN5 11 E1
Shedfield Way. NN4 21 F2
Sheep St. NN1 5 C2
Sheerwater Dri. NN3 9 H6
Sheffield Way. NN6 4 B3
Shelford Clo. NN3 9 F4
Shelley St. NN2 13 F2
Shelsley Dri. NN3 7 G5
Shepherd Clo. NN2 6 A5
Shepherds Wk. NN7 25 F3
Shepperton Clo. NN3 15 G2
Sheraton Clo. NN3 14 B1
Sheriff Rd. NN1 13 G4
Sherwood Av. NN2 6 A3
Shire Pl. NN3 9 F4
Shoal Creek. NN4 21 F4
Short La. NN7 23 D2
Shurville Clo. NN6 4 B3
Siddons Way. NN3 22 C2
Sidebrook Ct. NN3 8 D4
Silver St. NN1 5 C2
Silverdale Rd. NN3 14 B1
Silverstone Clo. NN2 6 D4
Sir John Pascoe Way.
NN5 11 E4
Siward Vw. NN5 11 F2
Skawle Ct. NN3 8 D6
Sketty Clo. NN4 18 D4
Skinner Av. NN5 16 A1
Skipton Clo. NN4 21 E1
Sladeswell Ct. NN3 15 E3
Smitherway. NN7 25 F3
Smyth Ct. NN3 8 D6
Snetterton Clo. NN3 7 F5
*Snowbell Sq, Willow
Brook Sq. NN3 15 G1
Somerset St. NN1 5 E1
Sotheby Rise. NN3 15 H1
South Bern. NN4 16 D3
South Bridge Rd. NN4 17 F2
South Copse. NN4 21 E2
South Holme Ct. NN3 8 C4
South Oval. NN5 11 H2
South Paddock. NN3 8 D5

South Portway Clo. NN3 8 D3
South Priors Ct. NN3 9 E6
South St. NN1 13 F5
South St. NN7 26 C4
South Ter. NN1 13 G5
South Vw. NN7 25 A2
Southampton Rd. NN4 17 F3
Southcrest. NN4 16 C5
Southcroft. NN3 8 A2
Southfield Av. NN4 17 F2
Southfield Rd. NN5 10 D6
Southwood Hill. NN4 16 D3
Spanslade Rd. NN3 15 E2
Spectacle La. NN3 7 F1
Spelhoe St. NN3 8 D3
Spencer Bridge Rd.
NN5 12 B5
Spencer Clo. NN6 4 C3
Spencer Haven. NN5 12 B4
Spencer Par. NN1 5 E3
Spencer Rd. NN1 13 E4
Spencer St. NN5 12 B6
Spenfield Ct. NN3 8 D6
Spinney Clo. NN2 6 D2
Spinney Dri. NN4 21 F4
Spinney Hill Cres. NN3 7 H5
Spinney Hill Rd. NN2 7 F6
Spinney Hill Rd. NN3 7 G5
Spinney Rd. NN3 7 H3
Spinney Way. NN3 7 H5
Spinneyside Wk. NN3 9 F5
Spring Clo. NN2 6 D1
Spring Gdns. NN1 5 E3
Spring Gdns. NN6 4 B3
Spring La. NN1 5 A1
Spring La. NN7 26 E1
Springbanks Way. NN4 17 E5
Springfield. NN4 22 A5
Springfield. NN7 26 E2
*Springfield Ct,
Birds Hill Rd. NN3 8 D6
Springwood Ct. NN3 8 D4
Spruce Ct. NN3 8 C6
Spyglass Hill. NN4 21 E2
Squires Wk. NN3 7 H6
Stable Ct. NN2 6 C6
Stafford Pl. NN3 7 G2
Stagshaw Clo. NN4 17 F6
Staines Clo. NN5 11 G6
Standens Barn Rd. NN3 14 D3
Standing Stones. NN3 9 F6
Stanfield Rd. NN5 11 E6
Stanford Way. NN4 17 F6
Stanhope Rd. NN2 12 D2
Stanley Rd. NN5 12 B5
Stanley St. NN2 12 C3
Stantion Av. NN3 7 H5
Starmers La. NN7 24 C4
Station Mews. NN3 15 G2
Station Rd. NN3 15 G2
Station Rd. NN6 4 A3
Station Rd,
Cogenhoe. NN7 23 A2
Station Rd,
Little Houghton. NN7 19 H2
Steene St. NN5 12 B5
Stenson St. NN5 12 B5
Stephen Bennet Clo.
NN5 11 E4
Stevens Ct. NN6 4 B2
Stevenson St. NN4 17 F3
Stewart Clo. NN3 22 A1
Stimpson Av. NN1 13 F4
Stirling St. NN5 11 H5
Stockley St. NN1 13 F5
Stockmead Rd. NN3 15 E3
Stockwell Av. NN4 21 G3
Stockwell Rd. NN7 20 C4
Stockwell Way. NN7 20 C4
Stoke Firs Clo. NN4 22 A5
Stone Circle Rd. NN3 8 C3
Stone Hill Ct. NN3 8 C6
Stone Way. NN5 11 E5
Stonebridge Ct. NN3 8 D6
Stoneleigh Chase. NN5 11 F3
Stonewold Clo. NN2 6 B5
Stoneyhurst. NN4 16 D3
Stour Rd. NN5 11 H6
Stourhead Dri. NN4 21 F1
Stowe Wk. NN3 7 F4
Stratford Dri. NN4 21 G2
Stratton Clo. NN3 14 B5
Strawberry Hill. NN3 9 G6
Streambank Rd. NN3 8 C3
Streatfield Rd. NN5 12 B5

Streeton Way. NN6 4 A2
Strelley Av. NN3 14 D3
Stuart Clo. NN4 16 C6
Stubble Clo. NN2 6 B4
Studland Rd. NN2 12 C2
Sulby Rd. NN3 8 C3
Sulgrave Rd. NN5 12 A4
Summerfields. NN4 16 B4
Summerhouse Rd. NN3 7 G3
Summit Rise. NN4 21 G1
Sunderland St. NN5 12 B5
Sundew Ct. NN4 16 B5
Sunningdale Clo. NN2 13 F1
Sunny Side. NN6 4 A3
Sunnyside. NN4 22 A6
Sunset Ct. NN3 15 E2
Sussex Clo. NN5 11 E6
Sutton Acre. NN7 26 F1
Sutton Bank. NN7 16 F1
Sutton Clo. NN2 7 E3
Sutton St. NN7 26 F2
Swain Ct. NN3 8 C6
Swale Dri. NN5 11 H1
Swallow Clo. NN4 20 D1
Swan St. NN1 5 D4
Swan Valley Way. NN4 16 A6
Swan Yd. NN1 5 C3
Swansea Cres. NN5 12 B4
Swansea Rd. NN5 12 B4
Swinford Hollow. NN3 15 E4
Sycamore Rd. NN5 11 E5
Symington St. NN5 12 B5
Syresham Way. NN2 6 D4

Taborley Clo. NN3 14 D3
Talan Rise. NN3 9 F4
Talavera Way. NN3 8 A3
Talbot Rd. NN1 13 F4
Tall Trees Clo. NN4 16 C6
Tallyfield End. NN4 16 C3
Tamar Clo. NN5 11 G2
Tamarisk Dri. NN3 8 A3
Tanfield La. NN1 14 A6
Tanglewood. NN4 21 G4
Tanner St. NN1 5 B4
Tansy Clo. NN4 16 B5
Tapley Gdns. NN4 21 F1
Tarn Croft. NN3 8 A6
Tarragon Way. NN4 21 G2
Tarrant Clo. NN3 22 C2
Tarrant Way. NN3 22 C2
Tate Gro. NN4 22 A4
Tattersall Clo. NN3 7 G5
Taunton Av. NN3 14 A4
Tavistock Clo. NN3 15 H1
Teal Clo. NN4 16 B6
Tebbutts Yd. NN6 4 B2
Teesdale. NN3 8 D3
Telford Way. NN5 16 A1
Templar Dri. NN2 6 B6
Ten Pines. NN3 8 D2
Tenby Rd. NN5 12 B5
Tennyson Clo. NN5 12 A3
Tenter Rd. NN3 7 F2
Teviot Clo. NN5 11 G2
Tewkesbury Clc. NN4 16 D4
Thames Rd. NN4 21 E1
Thatchwell Ct. NN3 14 D3
The Green. NN7 26 F2
The Ashes. NN4 22 C5
The Avenue. NN1 13 F6
The Avenue. NN2 6 A3
The Avenue,
Moulton. NN3 22 D3
The Avenue,
Spinney Hill. NN3 7 G6
The Avenue. NN5 11 H5
The Avenue. NN7 26 E2
The Bartons Clo. NN5 12 A3
The Briars. NN4 16 D3
The Causeway. NN3 15 G4
The Choakles. NN4 22 C5
The Close. NN2 6 D5
The Crescent. NN1 13 F3
The Crescent. NN3 22 C2
The Crescent. NN7 26 F1
The Croft. NN5 11 H3
The Cross. NN4 19 F3
The Drapery. NN1 5 C2
The Drive. NN1 13 F3
The Drive. NN5 10 D5
The Fairoaks. NN3 14 D3
The Glebe. NN1 26 E2
The Green Court Rd.
NN1 5 B4

The Green. NN2 6 C6
The Green, Brafield. NN7 23 B6
The Green, Great Houghton. NN4 19 F4
The Green, Hardingstone. NN4 18 A6
The Green, Kislingbury. NN7 24 D5
The Green, Nether Heyford. NN7 25 A2
The Greys. NN7 26 B2
The Grove. NN3 22 B1
The Hayride. NN4 20 D1
The Headlands. NN3 14 A3
The Hollies. NN3 22 A1
The Lakes. NN4 18 D2
The Laurels. NN3 22 A1
The Lawns. NN5 11 G4
The Leys. NN2 12 C1
The Mews. NN3 14 C3
The Motts. NN7 24 B2
The Nurseries. NN3 22 B2
The Orchard. NN7 24 C5
The Orchard. NN7 26 F2
The Paddocks. NN7 25 E4
The Parade. NN1 5 C2
The Pastures. NN2 6 B4
The Peak. NN7 25 B2
The Piece. NN7 23 C2
The Pyghtle. NN6 4 B2
The Riding. NN1 5 D3
The Rise. NN2 6 C6
The Scraplands. NN5 11 E6
The Smithy. NN3 14 C3
The Square. NN6 4 A3
The Vale. NN1 13 G2
The Warren. NN4 18 A6
The Weavers. NN4 21 F2
Thebwell Rd. NN3 14 D3
Thenford St. NN1 5 F2
Thirlestane Cres. NN4 17 E3
Thirlestane Rd. NN4 17 E3
Thirlmere Av. NN3 8 B6
Thistleholme Clo. NN2 13 F1
Thomas St. NN1 5 D1
Thorn Hill. NN4 16 D3
Thornapple Clo. NN3 9 G6
Thornburn Rd. NN3 14 C4
Thornby Dri. NN2 6 C6
Thornfield. NN3 9 F5
Thornton Clo. NN7 26 F2
Thornton Rd. NN2 12 C2
Thorpe Rd. NN4 17 F3
Thorpe Rd. NN6 4 B4
Thorpeville. NN3 8 B2
Thrupp Bridge. NN4 22 C6
Thruxton Dri. NN3 7 G5
Thursby Rd. NN1 13 H4
Thurspit Pl. NN3 15 G2
Thyme Ct. NN3 8 C6
Tideswell Clo. NN4 16 C6
Tiffany Gdns. NN4 21 F2
Tinsley Clo. NN3 9 F6
Tintern Av. NN5 12 B4
Tiptoe Clo. NN3 9 G6
Tithe Rd. NN7 26 A4
Titley Bank Av. NN6 4 B1
Tiverton Av. NN2 6 C2
Tollgate Clo. NN2 12 C1
Tollgate Way. NN5 11 F6
Toms Clo. NN4 21 F5
Tonmead Rd. NN3 8 C5
Tonmead Wk. NN3 9 E5
Topwell Ct. NN3 15 E2
Touraine Clo. NN5 10 C2
Towcester Rd. NN1 5 B4
Towcester Rd. NN4 17 E4
Towcester Rd. NN7 2 B4
Tower Field Sq. NN3 9 E3
Tower Hill Clo. NN4 16 C3
Tower St. NN1 5 B2
Townley Way. NN6 4 A2
Towton Ct. NN4 16 D4
Treetops. NN3 9 E4
Trent Clo. NN5 11 H2
Trevor Clo. NN5 11 G5
Trevor Cres. NN5 11 G5
Trimley Clo. NN3 14 B5
Trinity Av. NN2 13 E2
Triumph Gdns. NN5 10 C3
Trussel Rd. NN3 15 G2
Tudely Clo. NN4 22 B4
Tudor Rd. NN1 13 G2
Turn Furlong. NN2 6 B4
Turnberry La. NN4 21 E3
Turner St. NN1 13 F4
Tweed Rd. NN5 11 G6
Twigden Rd. NN7 24 C5
Twyford Clo.NN3 15 E4
Tybeck Ct. NN2 6 B6
Tyes Ct. NN3 8 D6
Tyne Rd. NN5 11 G6
Tyringham Clo. NN3 14 B2

Underbank Way. NN3 8 A3
Upland Rd. NN3 14 A1
Upper Bath St. NN1 5 B2
Upper High St. NN7 24 B2
Upper Mounts. NN1 5 D1
Upper Priory St. NN1 12 C4
Upper Thrift St. NN1 13 G5
Uppingham St. NN1 12 C4
Upton Clo. NN2 7 E4
Upton Way. NN5 16 A1

Valemead Wk. NN3 9 E4
Valentine Way. NN3 9 G6
Valley Cres. NN3 15 F2
Valley Rd. NN3 15 F2
Vantage Mdw. NN3 9 H6
Velocette Way. NN5 10 C2
Verdant Vale. NN4 21 G2
Vernon St. NN1 13 F5
Vernon Ter. NN1 13 F5
Vernon Wk. NN1 13 F5
Verwood Clo. NN3 8 D4
Vicarage Clo. NN2 6 B6
Vicarage La. NN2 6 B6
Vicarage Rd. NN5 12 B5
Victoria Clo. NN6 4 B2
Victoria Gdns. NN1 5 D4
Victoria Prom. NN1 5 D4
Victoria Rd. NN1 5 F2
Victoria Rd. NN7 23 C2
Victoria St. NN1 5 D1
Vienne Clo. NN5 10 B3
Vigo Ter. NN1 17 H1
Villaton Gdns. NN3 14 D3
Vincent Clo. NN5 10 C4
Viscount Rd. NN3 9 G3
Vokes Clo. NN3 15 E2
Vyse Rd. NN2 6 C2

Wade Mdw Ct. NN3 8 D5
Waggoners Way. NN7 25 F3
Wagtail Clo. NN3 8 A3
Waingrove. NN3 9 F5
Wakefield Rd. NN2 6 D5
Wakefield Way. NN7 25 B1
Wakehurst Rd. NN4 21 F1
Walbeck Clo. NN2 6 C5
Walgrave Clo. NN3 15 F3
Wallace Gdns. NN2 13 G1
Wallace Rd. NN2 13 G1
Wallace Ter. NN2 13 G1
Walledwell Ct. NN3 14 D3
Wallingford End. NN3 15 E4
Walton Heath Way. NN2 7 F6
Wantage Clo. NN3 22 C3
Wantage Rd. NN1 13 G4
*Wardington Ct, Welford Rd. NN2 6 C6
Wardlow Clo. NN4 16 C6
Warren Rd. NN5 12 A4
Warwick Clo. NN5 11 E4
Washbrook Clo. NN3 15 F2
Washington St. NN2 12 C1
Water La. NN4 22 A5
Watercross Clo. NN4 22 B5
Watering La. NN4 21 F5
Watermeadow Dri. NN3 8 D4
Waterpump Ct. NN3 8 D4
Watersmeet. NN3 14 A5
Watery La. NN7 25 B1
Watkin Ter. NN1 13 E4
Watling St. NN7 26 B1
Waveney Way. NN5 11 H3
Waverley Rd. NN2 13 F2
Waypost Ct. NN3 8 D6
Wayside Acres. NN4 17 E6
Weddell Way. NN4 18 D3
Wedmore Clo. NN5 11 F5
Weedon Rd, Duston. NN5 11 F6
Weedon Rd, Kislingbury. NN7 24 A4
Weedon Rd, Nether Heyford. NN7 25 A1
Weggs Farm Rd. NN5 10 B3
Welford Rd. NN2 6 A2
Well Yd. NN2 6 B6
Welland Grn. NN5 11 H2
Welland Wk. NN5 11 H2
Welland Way. NN5 11 H2
Wellingborough Rd. NN1 13 F5
Wellingborough Rd. NN3 9 E6
Wellingborough Rd. NN6 4 B1
Wellington St. NN1 5 D2
Wells Ct. NN3 22 B3
Wenlock Way. NN5 11 F3
Wensleydale. NN2 6 A4
Wentworth Way. NN2 13 F1
Wessex Way. NN3 14 A2
West Bank. NN3 8 C3
West End. NN7 25 D3
West Leys Ct. NN3 8 A2
West Mead Ct. NN3 15 E2
West Oval. NN5 11 H3
West Paddock Ct. NN3 8 D5
West Priors Ct. NN3 9 E5
West Ridge. NN2 6 D6
West Rising. NN4 21 G1
West St. NN1 13 F5
West St. NN3 22 A2
West St. NN6 4 A3
West St. NN7 26 B3
West Way. NN6 4 A2
West Way. NN7 26 B3
Westbury Av. NN5 11 F5
Westcott Way. NN3 14 C4
Westerdale. NN2 6 A4
Western Av. NN7 25 A2
Westfield Rd, Duston. NN5 10 D4
Westfield Rd, Northampton. NN5 11 H5
Westgate Rd. NN5 11 F6
Westleigh Clo. NN2 13 F4
Weston Mill La. NN3 14 C5
Weston Way. NN3 14 A3
Weston Wharf. NN1 5 B4
Westone Av. NN3 14 C2
Wetheral Clo. NN3 8 B5
Whaddon Clo. NN4 16 B4
Whaley Gro. NN7 23 C2
Wheatfield Gdns. NN3 13 H2
Wheatfield Rd. NN3 13 H2
Wheatfield Rd Nth. NN3 13 H2
Wheatfield Rd Sth. NN3 13 H2
Wheatfield Ter. NN3 13 H2
Whernside Way. NN5 11 F4
Whilton Rd. NN2 7 E5
Whistlets Clo.NN4 16 B5
Whiston Rd. NN2 6 D5
White Doe Dri. NN3 8 A2
White Hills Cres. NN2 6 C3
White Hills Way. NN2 6 C3
White Way. NN6 4 A2
Whitegates. NN4 16 A5
Whitehart Clo. NN3 15 F2
Whiteland Rd. NN3 14 A1
*Whitesands Way, Ashpole Spinney. NN4 16 A4
Whitfield Rd. NN5 11 E3
Whitfield Way. NN2 6 D4
Whiting Ct. NN3 22 A3
Whittlebury Clo. NN2 6 D4
Whittles Cross. NN4 22 C5
Whitworth Cres.NN6 4 B2
Whitworth Rd. NN1 13 F4
Wickery Dene. NN4 22 C5
Wilby St. NN1 13 G5
Wildern La. NN4 21 F3
Wilford Av. NN3 14 D3
William St. NN1 12 D4
Williton Clo. NN3 14 C4
Willow Brook Sq. NN3 15 G1
Willow Cres. NN4 19 F4
Willow La. NN4 19 F3
Willow Rise. NN3 15 F3
Willow Vw. NN7 24 C5
Wilson Way. NN6 4 B3
Wimbledon St. NN5 12 B5
Wimborne Clo. NN3 9 G6
Winchester Clo. NN4
Winchester Rd. NN4
Windermere Way. NN3
Windflower Pl. NN3
Windingbrook La. NN4
Windmill Ter. NN2
Windrush Rd. NN4
Windrush Way.NN5
Windsor Clo. NN7
Windsor Ct. NN3
Windsor Cres. NN5
Windyridge. NN2
Winnington Clo. NN3
Winsford Way. NN3
Winston Clo. NN3
Winston Clo. NN7
Wisley Clo. NN4
Wisteria Way. NN3
Witham Grn. NN5
Witham Way. NN5
Witham Way. NN5
Witton Rd. NN5
Woburn Gate. NN3
Wood Avens Clo. NN4
*Woodborough Gdns, Porchester Gdns. NN3
Woodcote Av. NN3
Woodford St. NN1
Woodhall Clo. NN4
Woodhill. NN1
Woodhill Rd. NN5
Woodland Av. NN3
Woodland Clo. NN5
Woodland Walk. NN3
Woodlands Grange. NN6
Woodley Chase. NN5
Woodpecker Way. NN4
Woodrush Way. NN3
Woodside Av. NN3
Woodside Cres. NN3
Woodside Grn. NN5
Woodside Way. NN5
Woolmonger St. NN1
Wootton Brook Clo. NN4
Wootton Hill Farm. NN4
Wootton Hope Dri. NN4
Worcester Clo. NN3
Wrekin Clo. NN4
Wrenbury Rd. NN5
Wychwood Clo. NN5
Wycliffe Rd. NN1
Wymersley Clo. NN4
Wysall Rd. NN3

Yardley Dri. NN2
Yarwell Sq. NN4
Yelvertoft Rd. NN2
Yeoman Dri. NN2
Yeoman Meadow Rd. NN4
Yew Tree Gdns. NN7
Yewtree Ct. NN3
York Av. NN7
York Rd. NN1

Edition 514B